Library of Congress Catalog Card No. 78-106385
ISBN 0-933112-00-9

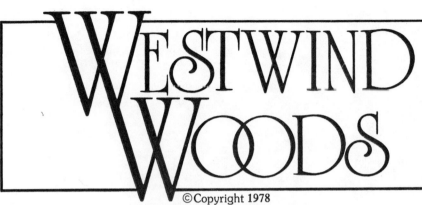

© Copyright 1978
Michigan United Conservation Clubs

by Thomas E. Huggler

Art Director • Ben Graham
Illustrated by • James Caulfield
Cover illustration • Dietmar Krumrey
Foreword • Ben East

Published by
Michigan United Conservation Clubs
Box 30235, Lansing, Mich. 48909

To Brian and Jennifer...in the earnest hope that the outdoor world will always be there for you to continually discover, to borrow and to give back in turn to your children.

TABLE OF CONTENTS

FOREWORD

In this book, Thomas E. Huggler and the Michigan United Conservation Clubs are undertaking to help with a job so big and vital that it should be the concern of every person in the nation—the job of interesting young readers in the problems of conservation and in helping to solve them.

The first step in persuading people, young or old, to respect and safeguard their outdoor heritage is to call to their attention the simple fact that woods, waters, wildlife and wild places exist and to point out the worth and importance of these resources to mankind. Until an adult or a youngster knows enough about a bird, animal, marsh or river to be interested in it, he is not likely to care what happens to it.

Between these covers, Tom Huggler is telling young readers something about the wild things that live in his chosen tract of woods, marsh, river and pond. He is relating how the birds and animals live, what makes them of interest and why they need certain measures of protection. Once his readers know these things, wildlife will never be beyond their fields of interest.

Today's young readers of "Westwind Woods" will be adults in a few more years, and many of them will be hunters and fishermen. If they know enough about the outdoors to understand and appreciate it, they will almost certainly also be concerned with safeguarding it from abuse.

It is the purpose of this book to help bring that about. The man who, as a boy, has learned where the woodcock nests and how the muskrat lives beneath the ice of his winter pond sees the outdoors and its wild denizens, as well as the woods and wetlands that are their home, through different eyes. Knowing something about them, there is little chance he will be indifferent to their well being.

I join the author and publisher of this book in the sincere hope that it attains at least a share of the goal they have set for it.

BEN EAST

Holly, Michigan
April 1978

CHAPTER 1

PHILO
the Woodcock

hilo stood up, moved and then sat tightly again to the clutch of eggs beneath her. The woodcock had warmed her nest of dried grass, twigs and dead leaves for nearly two weeks. A few more days would pass, though, before the four light cinnamon-colored eggs with dark brown spots would break open with new life.

She was glad for the warming sun of this windless afternoon in early May but looked forward to darkness again. Then her mate would leave his nap elsewhere in the alder thicket to probe in the warm, wet marsh border for fat earthworms. He had fed Philo several times nightly during her long stay with the eggs and was never far away.

The nearby 10-acre marsh was bursting with early spring life. Skunk cabbages pushed upward from rich, black earth. Yellow cowslips flanked a winding stream that trickled from greening woods to feed the marsh. The air was heady both with the smells of decaying vegetation and new plant growth that was overtaking everything.

Philo wiped her long, stem-like bill against the soft, warm earth and listened to Agel, the red-winged blackbird, as he poured forth a full-throated song. Perched atop a nodding cattail, Agel guarded their nest in a dogwood thicket while his mate swooped to the pond for a quick drink.

Elsewhere in the lively marsh, frogs of many types provided a constant croaking chorus to the grating calls of several grackles. The grackles were led by Cassidix, a male bird with yellow eyes and purple-green feathers. They nested in a small grove of poplars bordering the pond's marshy fringe. With wings locked and fan tails spread, they soared through the clear air like black paper airplanes. The noisy troop chatted back and forth with sounds like a rusted gate opening and closing.

Philo had returned to this same marsh and alder thicket twice before. She did not know that most of the other woodcocks that had migrated with her from the wintering grounds along the Atchafalaya River in Louisiana would journey farther north to build nests and raise young. Philo did not understand and could only obey the strange urge that each year guided her back to her birthplace.

She shifted again atop the crude nest and spread her wings to stretch them. Her mate, a second for Philo since her first was killed by a southern hunter during the previous fall migration, had chosen the nesting site. This is the woodcock custom.

The marsh and alder clump lay in the middle of Westwind Woods, a four-mile long by two-mile wide section of woods and meadows. The twisting Kenawabi River cut the tract lengthwise in two. The whole wild area was surrounded by a perimeter of asphalt highways. On the river's west bank, across from the marsh, farmers would soon plant wheat, soybeans and corn in mile-long rows that would begin at the highway and slope down to the river.

Downstream lay hardwood groves of oak, beech, maple and hickory for nearly two miles to the Grayson Road Bridge. A finger-like valley split the river bottoms from the marsh to the bridge and broke into long fields on the west bank and to gentle slopes of hardwoods on the east side.

The 10-acre marsh and pond across the barren fields dazzled like a blue-green gem in the late afternoon sun. Here, the alder thicket stood as a brief compromise between cattails and the hardwoods of the higher ground. Philo's nest was only one of three woodcock nests in the entire eight square mile area.

For three miles upriver from the marsh the Kenawabi River wound like a snake through woodlots and farmland. Giant sycamore and swamp maples put on fresh pastels of green as they sprouted fresh leaves. The hardier beech and oak trees that also grew along the river bottoms were peppered with red and maroon buds and would follow their greening neighbors in a few days.

The bustling community of Bellecrest, a small city of about 4,000 people, lay three miles upriver from the alder tangle where Philo nested. An old iron railroad bridge and a newer concrete highway bridge with thick stone abutments spanned the river in Bellecrest. For a mile downstream, riverside homeowners had cleared the tangled forest growth. Little man-made park areas lay behind most of the suburban homes. Sometimes, docks, storage sheds and rusted pipes that drew river water for watering lawns could be seen on both river banks.

Westwind Woods began where the brick and aluminum ranch style homes stopped. It continued downstream for two miles, past the marsh and alder thicket, and then went on for another two miles before ending at the Grayson Road Bridge. The only interruptions in the private tract were a few farms on the west bank and a half-mile long invasion of new homes called Riverside Subdivision on the east bank.

Philo's mate had followed her home to Westwind Woods weeks before during the spring migration. This land was new to him as he was reared in the northern grouse and woodcock country. He easily chose the nesting site as there were no other alder thickets for miles.

Although hastily built, the nest blended well with the dark floor of dead plant life and sticks. Only a careful eye could detect the nesting Philo whose gray forehead and three black head bands mixed well with her drab surroundings. Her needle-like, four-inch bill appeared to be just another twig along a piece of brown-gray wood.

The sun hung over the western horizon, beyond newly plowed, sterile fields. Jagged fence rows that flanked the fields were headed by white farmhouses and gleaming red barns. Philo heard the rapid flight of Sponsa, the wood duck, and his mate as they scurried low overhead returning to their nest near the muskrat houses. Cassidix and his noisy troop of grackles kept up their grating conversation, and the frogs peeped on loudly. Then, Philo heard a strange sound.

She listened carefully. Philo heard the foreign noises clearly now, young voices talking excitedly and the occasional yelp of a dog. Fearful, she squatted even more tightly to her clutch of eggs.

Three boys—Greg Thomas, Jerry Johnson and Steve Nisbet—had hiked to the pond after school. They hoped they might catch some tadpoles for their sixth grade science class. Only an hour before, the yellow school bus had unloaded them at their suburban homes in Riverside Subdivision, the deepest human thrust into Westwind Woods.

That morning in science class, the boys' teacher, Mrs. Rachel, had shown a filmstrip on how tadpoles turned into adult frogs. On the bus ride home, Jerry, a husky boy with football player shoulders, brought up the idea to catch some tadpoles for science class. His dark, unruly hair that tried to cover his broad forehead and two large ears dropped to healthy pink cheeks split by a ready smile. Jerry was far from being the top student in science class. To him, his idea sounded like a good way to avoid another F on his report card.

Greg had jumped on Jerry's suggestion. A smaller, handsome boy with black snapping eyes, long black hair and pecan-tinted skin, Greg was always ready for action. The two boys lived side by side in the new subdivision, and their fathers worked in the same automobile factory 10 miles away in Gratiot City.

Steve was a tall, quiet, more studious boy who was sometimes serious. He studied hard. His blonde hair lay close to his head and graced his forehead in generous bangs. Two bright blue eyes dominated a child's face with its slender nose, frail chin and light freckled cheeks.

Steve lived with his mother and younger sister in a brown brick home on the turnaround at the end of Riverside Subdivision. A 30-year-old uncle, his mother's younger brother, lived with the family. Uncle Ray taught ecology and wildlife courses at the university in Gratiot City. Steve's father had died in a helicopter crash during the Viet Nam war a few years before.

"I know where we can find some tadpoles," Steve had told the others.

"My Uncle Ray and I saw some last year in the marsh back in Westwind Woods."

Pixie, Greg's female Brittany spaniel, had begged to go with the boys, and Greg gave in although he thought she might frighten the frogs. A fast-paced mile hike along a twisting foot path brought them out to a break in the hardwoods. Here, cottonwood, sycamore and swamp maple gave way to the alder thicket where Philo lay very still.

The boys had watched the arrowing flight of Sponsa and his mate, and Jerry said that he'd have to tell his dad about the ducks nesting on the pond again. Jerry's dad had promised to take his son duck hunting next fall.

Steve, a full two months younger than either Greg or Jerry, led the way into the alder tangles with Pixie pushing just ahead of him.

"It's not too wet in here," he said. "The pond's just on the other side."

The others followed, passing on the subdued branches that Steve offered behind his back. High in his poplar branch, Cassidix spotted the intruders by now and sounded a rasping cry of alarm to the other grackles. Suddenly, Pixie grew stiff, her right foot shot up and her stub tail became a quivering knob.

"She's on point!" Greg shouted. "Maybe there's a pheasant in here. Hold, girl, hold!" he ordered, repeating what he had heard his father command many times.

The boys pressed close to Pixie, stiff at attention, her eyes riveted to the ground.

"What is it?" Jerry questioned. "I don't see anything."

Just then Philo blinked and gave herself away, so perfectly did she blend with the dead leaves and sticks.

"It's some kind of weird bird," Greg announced.

"I never saw anything like it," Jerry added. "Look at its long mouth."

Steve bent far over and looked carefully at Philo, whose heart was nearly throbbing out of her chest. "It's a woodcock," he said. "I know because my uncle shot one once. They're protected, and you have to have a license to hunt them."

Pixie could hold her point no longer and rushed forward. Philo was off her nest in a blur of frantic wings and a shrill whistle of alarm. She narrowly missed the gaping jaws of the excited Brittany. Twisting her way through the thick alders, she settled to earth 50 yards away.

The boys saw the light brown eggs at once, and Greg threw his arms around Pixie to keep the eager dog from thrusting her nose into the nest.

"Hey, eggs, you guys. Look, four eggs!" Greg said.

"I wonder how old they are?" Jerry asked. "Let's bust one open and see."

Steve cut in. "No! My uncle said never to bother a bird's nest. Don't even touch the eggs because the mother might not come back."

"We could take just one egg to Mrs. Rachel's class," Greg offered. "Maybe we could hatch it in the biology lab."

Again Steve refused. "We can't, you guys. It's against the law to rip-off bird eggs. Besides, the mother might not sit on the others. Then they'd die, too."

Greg could see Steve's argument, but convincing Jerry to leave the eggs alone was another matter. The boys argued for several minutes until Jerry realized the odds were going to stay two to one.

"Who wants those stupid eggs, anyway?" he grumbled.

A short while later, the sun dipped behind a big red barn and evening's chill began to edge the thickening light. Nervously, Philo flitted back to her nest. The boys, having found no tadpoles today, had left the marsh and were nearly home. The frogs were back in full chorus again and Ondrata, the muskrat, cut a widening wake as he slowly swam across the still pond.

Cassidix and his noisy troop sat hushed in their lofty perches and Ardea, the great blue heron, stood sentinel-like in the marshy shallows and listened for a nearby frog to dare peep again.

Philo settled gently over the cold clutch of eggs. Her body heat would soon warm the inch-long shapes. Luckily, the day had been warm; inside the shells, the tiny woodcocks with their life-supporting yolk sacks were still alive and would hatch on time.

Philo could not know that her eggs were alive. Neither did she know that this year they were thicker shelled and would not break before they hatched as they had done during her first two nesting seasons. The reason was that the deadly poison, DDT, had been banned in the state for several years. Farmers once widely used DDT to kill insects.

DDT and some other poisons do not easily decay and often stay in the soil and water for years. Insects sprayed with the poisons and other smaller animals, such as earthworms and snails, were in turn eaten by birds. As a result, many woodcocks, eagles, sea gulls and other bird species suffered poor nesting seasons because of the thin-shelled eggs they laid.

Woodcocks have few natural enemies. Hawks, owls and foxes generally leave them alone unless really hungry. With the DDT gone, Philo and her young would have good survival chances. That is, unless their shrinking habitat someday included the alder thicket.

Again, Philo could not understand these truths. She only knew that the terrible fear gripped her no more, and she was happy to brood over her eggs, shifting positions as she felt the need. The air grew colder as night came down.

Soon her mate fluttered from the dark sky, his welcome cry of **Peent, Peent, Peent** piercing the night. He dropped a still sluggish earthworm before her and watched her throw back her head to devour the morsel.

CHAPTER 2

BRANTA
the Canada Goose

 ummer was winning the battle of the seasons in Westwind Woods. The longer days in early June provided more sunlight, which meant warmer temperatures and more growing time for plant life. The Kenawabi River returned to its normal flow, well below her banks once more. It would not flood again until the September rains. Heat waves shimmered over the pond during warm afternoons, but at dusk a slight chill filled the air. Still, day by day summer gained the upper hand over spring.

The growth and greening process begun in early May was now stepped up. On all sides, marsh grass and green-stemmed cattails with brown velvet heads nearly blotted out the pond whose surface was spattered with wide lily pads and their bright yellow flowers. The once bare sycamore, oak, maple and hickory trees now sported full heads of leaves. Across the pond and river foot-high rows of corn threatened soon to cover the barren earth there. This delighted a family of cottontail rabbits that already sampled the tender shoots each night.

To the careful eye at dusk, when most animals move about, Westwind Woods in June was a cradle of wildlife. Philo's eggs had hatched on time. In the cool evenings, she and her mate led four baby woodcocks, already half-sized carbon copies of their parents, on worm hunting trips. When the sun went down, bats flitted over the pond and picked out their supper from a smorgasbord of flying insects that swarmed about.

Ondrata was proud of his and his mate's first litter. He could often be seen watching the young muskrats play among lengthening shadows over

the pond. Cassidix's troop of grackles had multiplied and now fully occupied the small poplar grove along the marsh.

The offspring of Agel, the red-winged blackbird, had hatched and now kept their parents busy with food-providing chores. Everywhere in the woods, fields and marsh animals and their kind seemed abundant.

Other wildlife, however, had not fared as well this spring. A hungry raccoon had raided the nest of one of the mallard families on the pond, leaving only two eggs to replace the parent birds. Ardea, the mate-less great blue heron, had no replacement in Westwind Woods. She stalked the shallows alone at dusk. Corvus, the crow, and some of his black-feathered comrades had found the nest of Otus, the screech owl. After chasing their hated little enemy away from his hollow tree home, they smashed his eggs with pecks of their strong beaks. Otus and his mate would not raise young this year as June was too late to begin a new nest.

Just as new life was beginning for many animals of Westwind Woods, so an old way of life was ending, at least for the summer, for Steve and his friends. Jerry had been counting school days since Easter, weeks before. Now only three marks remained on the little calendar at his bedroom desk.

On one of those warm, muggy afternoons in early June, Steve jumped off the yellow school bus as it stopped on the turnaround in Riverside Subdivision. As usual, he told his friends he would see them later. Then he sprinted up the driveway to his mother's suburban home.

Steve was glad to see Uncle Ray's car in the drive. Maybe his uncle would go with him to see how the red-headed woodpecker's family were doing. Steve had found the red-head's nest in a dead elm near the river weeks before and had often watched the parent birds feed their young. He knew from pictures in one of his uncle's books that the little birds were ready to fly. That was one lesson he didn't plan to miss.

Theresa, his six-year-old sister, a kindergartner in the morning session at Steve's school, played with her favorite doll on the front steps.

"Hi, Sis. Uncle Ray's here already, isn't he?" Steve asked as he opened the door.

Voices of Steve's mother and her brother came from the kitchen. Steve guessed they were drinking coffee at the table near the patio doors that overlooked their wooded backyard and the river.

"I don't like it," Steve heard his uncle say, "and personally, I don't think it's a good idea, Ellen."

"Yes, but think of it, Ray," Steve's mother said. "A beautiful lake right in our own backyard. That would be great recreation for the whole county."

Steve popped into the kitchen.

"Hi, honey," she said. "How'd school go today?" Ellen Nisbet was a small-waisted, attractive woman in her mid-thirties. Her dark brown, curly hair and brown eyes were more like her daughter than her blue-eyed, blonde-haired son.

"What's this about a lake in our backyard?" Steve ventured, looking at his uncle.

Ray Moore flinched and looked out the window at the beech and maple trees that sloped to the river. Steve studied his uncle as Ray stared outside, his hand clenched tightly about a coffee mug. People often said that Steve looked like his uncle. Steve never could understand that. Except for the blue eyes and light-colored hair, there was nothing similar, Steve felt. His uncle was a big man, over six feet tall, with straight shoulders and a wide chest that tapered to a flat stomach and athletic thighs. Steve knew he would never be as big as his uncle when he grew up.

"They want our woods, Stevie," Ray finally said. "They want to cut down the trees and dam the river to make a lake."

"You mean just here in our backyard?" Steve wondered. Ellen got up to refill the coffee mugs.

"They want to cut it all down," Ray said evenly. "All of it—the whole Westwind Woods—and make a huge, man-made lake. Take out the old bridge at Grayson Road and put in a new roadway dam. Old Man West would flip in his grave if he knew that."

Ray did not say anything else and went back to staring out the window. Steve went up to his room to change. He knew the story of Colonel West and the Westwind Woods and he thought about it as he slipped into denim jeans. Colonel West was a wealthy man who had built automobile factories in Gratiot City 60 or 70 years before. He had also fought in the First World War after the factories began stamping out cars.

The Colonel had been a popular man in the county before his death. He had donated money and land so that people could learn things and enjoy themselves through recreation. Next year, as a seventh grader, Steve would attend West Junior High, one of many buildings named for the famous man.

The bachelor colonel had owned much land in the county, including the tract he called Westwind Woods. He had built a massive white frame house near a meadow and the hardwoods across from the many farms. When the old man died, he left Westwind Woods and the now boarded mansion to the Bellecrest County Parks and Recreation Commission. Colonel West had an early interest in conservation. He had allowed only controlled hunting on his lands and had protected them against poachers and trespassers.

Colonel West had not given the county parks group any direction as to what to do with the land when he died a decade earlier. Although many proposals had been made over the years, the eight square mile tract of woods and meadows, marshes and ponds remained in its wild state.

"Don't get me wrong, Ellen," Steve heard his uncle say "I'm all for recreation, and Lord knows we need parks and lakes badly in this county. But Westwind Woods is the only big piece of natural land left in this part of the state. I don't want to see it destroyed!"

"How do you know they want to make a lake here for sure?" Ellen asked.

"My students heard it on the radio this morning," Ray said. "The Bellecrest County Board met last night and approved the park commission's suggestion."

His uncle's voice flashed anger, and Steve knew it would be better to say nothing at this time. Steve quietly slipped through the kitchen and went out to the garage. He planned to check on the red-headed woodpecker and tell Uncle Ray about it later.

The days slipped by, soon school was over and hot summer weather descended on the county and Westwind Woods. Steve spent his time mowing neighbors' lawns for spending money and riding his bike, along with his friends into Bellecrest for midday dips in the community pool. Ray Moore began teaching a number of summer courses at the university in Gratiot City.

By midafternoon on the hottest June days, tree toads droned in a high-pitched buzz throughout Westwind Woods. The Kenawabi River dropped a few more inches and algae began dimpling the pond. One morning late in the month, Branta, the Canada goose, led his mate and their five goslings through marsh grass to the cool pond for a ducking.

Branta had been raised in Westwind Woods and had returned many times to nest with his life-long mate, a smaller, younger goose, a number of seasons. Canada geese did not normally nest in the region, passing up the small pond and marsh for wilder, more remote nesting grounds as far north as the Arctic Circle. But Branta's parents had been planted here years ago as a conservation project by two groups—the Bellecrest County Conservation Club and the Gratiot City Chapter of Ducks Unlimited. They wanted to build a local nesting colony of Canada geese, and they had been successful. After their clipped wings grew new flight feathers, the original geese had gone elsewhere. But Branta and a half dozen other nesting pairs of Canada geese returned here each spring.

Branta's five goslings had hatched several weeks before and the little yellow, fuzzy birds were already shedding their down for adult feathers. Their nest, a mound of grass, reeds, twigs and weeds, was lined with down plucked from the parent birds. It sat atop an old muskrat house. Now the young birds slept between the protective adults on dry land along the marsh edge.

Other Canada geese that nested on various grass-covered islands in the Kenawabi River sometimes lost a baby to huge northern pike. The submarine-like pike sulked beneath sunken logs in deep pools of the river and waited for such tasty morsels as young ducks and geese to paddle by overhead. Branta and his mate had wisely chosen their nesting site in the marsh because no such predators lived here or in the pond. Now the foot-high youngsters were too large a target for pike in the river, should the family happen to travel there.

Branta led the way into the pond, his gray-brown body buoyant like an oversized cork. The youngsters followed eagerly, five in a row, their little dark-colored, webbed feet propelling them along and bobbing in their father's wake. Branta's mate followed the brood.

It was midmorning when Branta heard the engine of a four-wheel drive pickup as it bounced along the river bank and stopped at the small stream that drained the pond. Branta had heard engine sounds before, from outboards of fishermen and duck hunters on the river. He connected these motor sounds with the dreadful humans. He stretched his long black neck high above the pond grasses and watched as three men sprang from the truck 100 yards away. He and his mate then quickly herded their young between them and slipped deeper back into the marsh. The only other hiding place was in the deep woods, and they offered little protection.

"The boss wants some measurements here, Joe," said a man dressed in faded blue coveralls and a plastic yellow hat. "This should be the lowest spot in the area."

"Take the transit right into the marsh and set up," a bare-shirted, deeply tanned young man said. "Joe and I will give you a reference point along the top of that low hill over there."

Donning hip waders, the first man slung a long-legged tripod over his shoulder and walked into the marsh. In his other hand he carried a worn clipboard that held papers full of drawings and numbers. A pencil tied to a cord was attached.

Jumping across the small stream, his partners circled the marsh and headed for a low hill a quarter of a mile to the east.

The surveying crew had been taking measurements throughout Westwind Woods all week long. Here and there along the river banks and hills on either side of the river they studied the land. Their wedge-shaped stakes of new cut lumber flashed in the summer sun, and thin orange plastic ribbons fluttered in the wind. The man named Joe and his deeply tanned companion carried several such stakes, a small sledge hammer and another clipboard.

From the marsh edge in a foot of water, the first man set up his transit. He spread the three legs wide for support in the soft bottom. Then he waved to his partners on the hill and together they began taking measurements and writing down figures. Their voices crackled over walkie-talkies as they discussed their findings.

"The way I figure it," the man in the marsh said after several minutes, "the deepest spot in the lake would be about 18 feet right here."

"Strike another angle to make sure," the man named Joe answered over the walkie-talkie.

"I'll have to move up into the marsh to do that," came the response. "Just a minute."

Branta and his family had slipped as deeply into the marsh as possible. The parent geese crouched low to the wet reeds and huddled their brood between them. Branta could see the surveyor coming toward him, whistling and carrying his transit over his shoulder. His boots made sucking sounds as he slogged through the marsh, and the cattails fell away to either side of his wet, rubber hip waders.

Protecting his young against both people pressure and animal intruders was nothing new to Branta. Already this spring he had startled a family of mushroom pickers when they came too close to his nesting mate. And just last week he had chased away a prowling house cat. Now, he tensed for the attack.

The man stopped 10 feet away and was just unloading his transit when Branta lunged from the thick marsh grass. With wings spread wide and neck curled in a sinister-looking S shape, Branta ran up to the shocked man and began hissing loudly at him.

"What the devil!" the man hollered, dropping his transit. He tried to run but not before Branta snapped at him, striking his leg through the thick rubber protection.

"What's with you, you crazy goose?" the man stammered from a safe place several yards away. "I'm not trying to hurt you." The man started back for his transit, but Branta began to hiss and honk loudly. Beating his wings in defiance, the angry goose dared the man to come closer.

Over the walkie-talkie came loud laughter, and then a voice said, "Hey, what's the problem? Why don't you pick on someone your own size?"

"This crazy goose must have a nest or something in here," the man snapped back. "I'm coming over until things cool down."

Branta strutted about and pecked hard once or twice at the transit lying in the marsh grass. Stretching his neck high, he watched the man disappear into the reeds.

Only then did Branta return to where his family still froze huddled together, just as he had left them.

CHAPTER 3

FALCO
the Sparrow Hawk

fter fussing over his five youngsters and certain that they were all right, Branta strutted toward the Kenawabi River. The proud goose was still angry over his encounter with the surveyors. He held his head high above the marsh reeds and watched for any sign of the men. The little geese waddled after their father in a single line, and Branta's mate protected the rear. In the river shallows during this bright June day, the goslings could safely chase each other and bob for tidbits while their parents watched from shore. Branta's family would not be molested by humans anymore today.

Meanwhile, across the river a small, colorful bird perched high on a power line at the far end of a young soybean field. On the nearby highway cars whizzed by in both directions. Their tires hummed on the warm asphalt.

Every now and then, a big semitrailer, its stacks belching diesel smoke, roared by. Sometimes exhaust fumes blew past the little bird in a rush of wind that ruffled his handsome feathers.

But Falco, a two-year-old male sparrow hawk, paid little attention to the traffic below. Perched on his favorite hunting spot, about midway between two sprawling farms, Falco was used to the noises and fumes of a busy highway.

Sparrow hawks were common in Westwind Woods. They were one of the few wild creatures that actually thrived in living quarters close to human beings. More sparrow hawks are alive today than ever before. Not a lover of deep woods, the little hawks prefer open fields and farmlands where they hunt mice and grasshoppers as well as other small mammals and insects.

These birds are at home in villages like Bellecrest, where they have been

known to nest in peaks and eaves of houses. They even live on the outskirts of major American cities like Gratiot City. The sparrow hawk's ability to change eating habits quickly and to nest nearly anywhere it can find a suitable spot are two reasons for its abundance near human populations.

The little predators are generally left alone by other wild creatures. In fact, most of their losses come from human beings. Many sparrow hawks are killed each year by people who shoot them out of ignorance or hatred because they are birds of prey. Others die in traffic because of their habit of hunting near roads.

It seems strange that the sparrow hawk's chief helper, mankind, is also his worst enemy. But such is often the case in the delicate life and death struggle of wild things as they compete with human beings for living space.

Falco was actually a falcon, not a hawk. His streamlined shape and long, pointed wings, typical of a true falcon, made him faster than any hawk. The proper name for these birds is American kestrel, but most people call them sparrow hawks because of their small size and hawk-like predator habits.

Falco was a handsome bird. His breast was light tan color with dark, vertical streaking, and his wings were a deep blue-gray. Overall, about the size of a robin, Falco was much more striking in appearance. His crown was both blue-gray and red, and he had light and dark markings on the back of his head. Falco's notched, sharp beak made him appear fierce and noble.

The sparrow hawk perched on this same wire every day to watch for mice and insects moving in the roadside grass and field below. Feeding his mate and their four always hungry offspring was a constant chore for Falco. Already that morning he had delivered a number of grasshoppers which the mother bird had torn apart for their two-week-old infants. Now Falco wanted something bigger, a fat field mouse, perhaps.

All hawks and owls have tremendous eyesight. Falco was no exception. His eyesight was several times better than any man's and was far superior to others in the animal world except other birds of prey. Like a radar screen, Falco moved his head from side to side as he searched for strange movement in the waving grass. Suddenly, one eye caught something out of place, and he turned around on the power line to see what it was.

A foot-long garter snake had squirmed from the weed-choked ditch to the asphalt edge and was about to cross the two-lane highway. The snake was a big prize for the four-ounce bird but was just the change in diet that Falco was looking for. He dropped quickly from the wire and, with the thrill of attack in his brain, homed in for the kill.

The snake was stretching itself across the warm pavement when Falco nailed it in midsection. The little hawk drove his tiny, razor-sharp talons into the snake's scaly hide. Squirming in pain, the reptile whipped its flattened head around and struck its attacker. The blow knocked Falco off balance, and he released his hard grip. Wriggling frantically, the snake gained a few more inches of freedom before Falco again pounced on him.

Falco soon found that he could not lift the squirming snake as the reptile was both too heavy and too clumsy to carry. Angry, the sparrow hawk tried to drag his prize to the road edge. Here he might rip it apart and carry it home piece by piece. The snake still squirmed in an effort to get away, but

Falco hammered at it with his sharp beak and tried to half drag, half lift the reptile off the road. Inch by inch, the sparrow hawk was gaining.

In the other lane a huge truck and trailer roared by. Frightened, Falco let loose of the snake, and a blast of wind tumbled him over to the road's shoulder. As he stood half-dazed along the highway, another vehicle, this time a red station wagon, sped past in the other direction. Falco most surely would have been killed, as many sparrow hawks are each year, by the speeding car had he not been blown to the roadside. Instead of him, the car battered the snake.

Still confused, Falco flew back to his power line perch and watched for several minutes as other cars pounded the snake flat. The sparrow hawk sensed that he had just escaped a terrible danger and would not return to the road again for his prey. This lesson he would remember all his life.

After a while, Falco dropped from the wire perch and hovered on tippling wings over the green soybean field. He would take any game now as he knew the young birds, nesting in an old beech a quarter mile away, would be hungry. Soon, he spotted a fat grasshopper and, with a shriek of **killee, killee,** Falco dropped to earth. He swept the green 'hopper into tightly clenched claws and arched back up toward the blue sky and cottony clouds.

Falco did not know that his mate had grown impatient waiting for the food provider. She had left their nest in a small hollow cavity in the ancient beech tree. Falco and his mate, a much larger, though less colorful bird, had simply taken over an abandoned woodpecker's nest there.

The beech was one of several mature trees that grew in the middle of the wide soybean field. For some unknown reason, the one-acre stand of hardwoods had survived the farmer's ax years ago and was now home to a family of fox squirrels and a handful of birds. It was here that Falco raced with the dead grasshopper pinched in his claws.

Moments before, when Falco's mate had left the nest to find food, two hungry crows on lazily flapping wings approached the woodlot. Corvus, the crow, and his mate knew a smart trick to get food fast. It was an old game that the black pair had worked many times before. One of the birds would fly low, as a decoy, over a grove of trees to pull nesting birds from their broods. When the smaller, parent birds swarmed after the invading crow, they would not see his partner duck into the woods. With his strong beak, the killer crow would stab every egg he found. It made no difference if the eggs were hatched as raiding crows did not mind killing a nest full of youngsters. Later, at another grove the outlaw pair would change places.

Corvus hung back a hundred yards or so while his mate flew into the small grove. In answer to her caws, a half-dozen angry birds gave immediate chase. Corvus' mate was not worried. She could easily escape the angry songbirds by dodging and somersaulting, although this time a wood thrush got in a couple of skin-breaking raps.

Looking for an untended nest, the sharp-eyed Corvus slipped silently through the leafy branches. As he passed close to the giant beech where the sparrow hawks lived, he heard noises, a muffled chirping from within. Corvus dropped softly to a gnarled gray limb just below the neat round hole that marked the den entrance.

When the young sparrow hawks heard Corvus outside, clamoring to get a better look at the treasure he had just found, they opened up with loud cheeping. They thought the crow was one of the parent birds returning with food.

In his excitement, Corvus was having a hard time getting a grip on the smooth-skinned beech. His crooked feet kept slipping, but he finally managed to thrust his black head into the small, round hole. Just then Falco flew over and spotted Corvus trying to kill his offspring.

The sparrow hawk acted from instinct. He had to protect his young. He dropped the grasshopper in midair and, with an ear-piercing scream, dive-bombed the unknowing crow. Corvus never had a chance to slay any of the young sparrow hawks. When Falco's talons neatly sliced open his feathered back, Corvus popped his head from the hole and bawled loudly in pain.

Corvus was stunned. He did not know what had attacked him. He fell to the branch below and jerked his head about trying to see what had attacked him. Falco, furious and bent on killing this black intruder, swept up in a graceful arch and curved back for a second attack. This time, Corvus saw him coming in another dive-bomb. A couple of black feathers floated down as the crow leaped into the air to escape. He neatly dodged the attacking sparrow hawk as Falco shot past, screaming **killee, killee!** But the unlucky crow did not see Falco's mate, and she slammed into him with more force than Falco had.

Corvus knew he had to get out of the woodlot or be ripped apart. Angry, bleeding and missing some feathers, he dodged around trees with the little hawks on his tail feathers. Falco and his mate did not stop at the woodlot's edge. They chased the wounded crow, all the way tearing at him, across the soybean field nearly to the river.

Much time would pass before Corvus went egg-stealing again.

Triumphant, the sparrow hawks returned to their nest and checked their four youngsters who were still alive and still hungry. They had no idea how close to death they had come. Falco's mate slipped into their hollow home to quiet them, and the male bird flew out to the soybean field to hunt once more.

Moments later, a power swoop—made a bit more fancy because of his victory over the hated Corvus—turned up a fat field mouse, and Falco winged home with supper.

CHAPTER 4

the Cross Fox

he warm spell of late June continued into early July, and all of Westwind Woods lay heat shocked under day after day of boiling sun. The long corn rows in dry fields across the river had ceased their shooting growth. Now, browning leaves and plump ears of ripening corn with silk tassles began to form on green-brown stalks.

Farmers spraying and cultivating in the long fields of corn, soybeans and other crops raised great clouds of dust that could be seen for a long way. The bright green leaves that covered the forested parts of Westwind Woods began to droop by midmorning in need of water. On the pond, thick algae spread to shore, and the short grasses of the nearby meadow began to turn brown from the constant heat.

Rain was needed to reawaken Westwind Woods. Instead, each new day brought another deep blue sky and fleecy white clouds. Westwind Woods lay locked in a midsummer drought.

Most of the animals lived less active lives during such hot periods. Cassidix, the grackle, and his troop of black noisemakers were content to perch lazily on their poplar tree roosts. Painted turtles sunned themselves on logs both in the pond and along the shore of the shallow Kenawabi River. Branta, the Canada goose, and his growing family hung back in shaded areas near the river, and Sponsa, the wood duck, and his mate tried to teach their young to fly in the cooler evenings.

The surveying crews slowed their pace. The tanned men with bright yellow hard hats often took work breaks under shady oaks and maples. And yet more and more wooden stakes with orange plastic ribbons dotted the

slopes and meadows of Westwind Woods. Also, the men began to mark some trees with blue paint, especially the hardwoods near Grayson Road Bridge. A massive cutting program was expected to begin there in August.

In late afternoon when the bright sun sank behind wilting grain fields, some animals began to stir. At dusk, for example, several white-tailed deer would ease into the open meadow from hiding places in the hardwoods to munch what sweet summer grass they could find. They were plump animals with reddish-brown coats, including the fawns, which were fast losing their white baby spots. The deer were led by a wise old swamp buck. Odo was a heavy antlered deer that had escaped many seasons of hard hunting by hunters who wanted to collect his handsome horns.

With some of the animals it was difficult to tell parent from offspring as the youngsters had nearly reached full size. The young woodcocks were learning to fly and catch fat earthworms nearly as well as their parents. In two months at summer's end, they would leave Philo and her mate and wing south for the winter. Soon, Falco would not have to work as hard at food-gathering chores since his four youngsters were already testing their wings. Soon, they would try their skill at hunting. Ondrata, the muskrat, was about to begin a new litter with his mate. Their first-born had grown up and were gone.

A family of red foxes also began to move about in late afternoon. The parents, a crafty old male and a straw-colored vixen, had enlarged an old woodchuck hole to make their den. The den was at the crown of a low slope that rose above the river across from a few trees and the big meadow.

The old pair had raised other families here. Their den location was a good one because mice were abundant in Westwind Woods and provided food for their growing families. Besides, few people bothered the foxes since their den was located in the heart of the wild tract.

One person who knew about the foxes was a kindly farmer. He sometimes stopped his dark green tractor in the nearby cornfield to watch the animals. Homer Greene was an ancient, wrinkled, red-faced farmer who usually dressed in faded blue overalls and wore a shapeless brown felt hat. He would shut his tractor off and wait patiently for the little foxes to play near their riverside den. Homer chuckled softly to himself as the eager pups wrestled with one another and tried to catch grasshoppers in weeds along the slope.

Many people do not look kindly on red foxes because of a belief that they raid farmers' chicken coops and kill the poultry. Others insist that foxes slaughter wild rabbits and pheasants all year long, seriously hurting their numbers and causing lean hunting years. These beliefs resulted in a bounty system on foxes in many states. Until a few years ago when most bounties were stopped, thousands of foxes were turned in each year for the reward.

Studies of red fox diets proved that the animals eat mostly small rodents, like mice and rats. Only rarely will they kill a pheasant or rabbit for food. This evidence was the main reason that the bounty system was dropped.

Farmer Greene chuckled about the outdated bounty system. He had been a good friend of Colonel West before the old gentleman died and had bought his farmland from him many years before. Farmer Greene knew the Colonel was against the bounty system and the bad practice of den digging that it caused. Whenever Farmer Greene watched red fox pups play, he thought of the time that Colonel West caught a man on his property without permission.

The Colonel might have let the trespasser go with a stern warning, but the poacher had a blood-stained burlap sack of freshly killed fox pups. He planned to turn them in for reward. Instead, his reward was a stiff fine from the judge for trespassing.

One simmering late afternoon in mid-July, the old male fox slipped from his den to begin a night of hunting. He had been hunting longer hours than usual this summer and not because little food was available. His large family of seven pups needed much food, and the parents worked hard to meet that demand.

The old fox was trap-shy and hunter-wise as a result of many experiences with human beings. He had lost two toes on his right front foot as a young adult when he stepped into a baited trap. He had also been shot at by hunters a few times over the years. Once he even had felt the hot sting of shotgun pellets in his flesh. These experiences made him a cautious, smart animal.

The old male had seen populations of his kind grow and shrink over the years. The open farmland and semi-wooded sections of Westwind Woods and other nearby rural areas were perfect for foxes. But the bounty sometimes had cut deeply into their numbers. When bounties were dropped, foxes increased. Fewer hunters and trappers went after them then, though, because the fur was worth only three or four dollars for a long time. Now, the pelts were valuable, and increasing numbers of hunters and trappers followed their sport.

Trapping and hunting are good conservation. Foxes have no natural enemies, and without careful harvesting they can increase to a dangerous level.

In some areas, where hunting and trapping pressure is light, or in years past when the fur was nearly worthless, foxes overran an area. The result was widespread distemper, a disease that affects the nervous system. Another problem when there are too many foxes is mange, a condition in which the animals become sick and lose their hair. Trapping and hunting are good business, when done legally, because they keep foxes from overbreeding.

When the old male came out of the den, he tested the air for danger scents. Below the den lay the twisting Kenawabi River, its shallow brown water slowed to a crawl. The old fox barked once to his mate, still in their den, and trotted up the hill to the cornfield where he might catch something.

His vixen popped from the den and then, one by one, the seven pups rolled out to play. The little foxes were 10 weeks old and about ready to learn hunting skills. About half the size of their mother, the young reds were not lean like her but were still fat with puppyhood. And like puppies, they nipped at each other and wrestled together while the vixen tried to keep them collected in her mind.

All of the fox pups had soft, reddish-brown fur and were about the same size except one. This was Vulpes, a large male whose coat was becoming quite different than his brothers' and sisters'. Vulpes was a color phase of the orange-brown red fox breed. Along his back an almost black cross-shaped patch of hair began to form. This marked Vulpes as a cross fox.

Cross foxes were somewhat rare and often more valuable than the usual red fox. When Vulpes grew older, he would be much sought after by hunters and trappers.

The vixen, always on the alert for danger, ambled down the slope to the river for a drink. Several of the pups tumbled after her.

About this time, Steve and his Uncle Ray were hiking on the winding foot path along the river. Ray figured the old fox den would probably be in use again this year, and he wanted to get some pictures of any pups he could find. He carried a bright orange, aluminum frame backpack that bulged with a pair of cameras, tripod and several lenses.

He had asked Steve to come along because he knew his young nephew would be quiet and would not spook the foxes if any were using the den. Also, he knew how much Steve had grown to love the outdoors.

"Man, they've really got this area staked out, haven't they, Uncle Ray?" Steve asked as he tried to copy his uncle with long strides.

"Yes, Stevie, they do," Ray said, noting the wedge-shaped markers along the river banks. "It won't be long now before they start cutting down the big timber near the bridge." Ray had been mulling the problem over in his mind for a long time now and had been thinking about doing something—just what, he had not decided.

Whispering and walking softly, the two hid behind a storm-toppled maple across the river from the fox den. Ray set up his camera while Steve watched the easy to see den entrance 100 yards away.

"I know they're using the den, Uncle Ray," he whispered. "I know because fresh dirt is piled up around the hole."

Ray beamed approval. Steve certainly was learning all about the outdoors and animal habits. Ray was proud of his nephew.

The two soon caught a glimpse of a fox pup as it tumbled down the hill from a friendly butt given by the bigger Vulpes. When Ray saw the cross fox pup a few minutes later, he got very excited and began snapping many pictures.

"This is pretty rare, Steve," he said. "Everybody around will be out to bag him. He'll have to smarten up fast."

After a time, Farmer Greene's tractor chugged along the hilltop at the field's edge. The vixen yapped a warning, and the seven pups scurried into their den for safety.

Homer Greene was spraying his cornfield and did not dare stop, with night coming on, to wait for the foxes to resume play. The two photographers across the river watched Farmer Greene. Jets of vapor-like smoke curled above and behind the tractor and mixed with a cloud of dust to settle on the cornstalks.

"What's he spraying?" Steve wondered.

"I don't know," Ray said. "Probably spraying for smut or blight or something that attacks corn."

"Isn't that dangerous for the animals?"

"It depends on what it is," Ray said. "Some of that stuff, like Malathion and Silvex, is pretty potent. There are hundreds of insecticides and other poisons on the market for anybody to buy. And, yes, they can harm wildlife."

Ray then went on to explain how certain poisons sprayed on plants and crops can get into the natural food chain. Insects and small animals and birds eat the sprayed plants and seeds and become infected with the poison. Predators, in turn, kill the smaller birds and mammals for food and sometimes pick up the same poison. Many get sick and die.

"The worst killer was DDT," Ray said, "because it stayed in the soil and water for years. Luckily, it's been against the law to use DDT for many years now. But some of this other stuff is pretty bad, too."

Moments after Farmer Greene passed on and the big clouds of dust and spray had settled, Vulpes popped from the den entrance. His mother gave him a sharp nip for going out ahead of her. Soon, all the pups were out of the hole again.

Ray kept snapping pictures, but the light was going fast, the sun having sunk with Farmer Greene's clouds of dust and spray. Just then, the old male appeared on top of the hill. Hanging from his mouth was a small animal.

"A rabbit," Ray whispered excitedly. "Look, Steve, he caught a rabbit for the pups to eat!" Ray got in two or three good pictures of the father fox delivering a small cottontail for supper and the young foxes tearing into the kill.

Then it was too dark for good photography. Ray and Steve tucked away the equipment and began a brisk walk. They had to cover the two-mile hike home before complete darkness shut down on Westwind Woods.

The old male fox did not stop to watch his pups eat. He trotted over the hill, a dusky figure in the failing light, his long plume of a tail straight out. He knew the growing family needed more food. He would catch something for himself after they were fed.

Then, as though he had changed his mind, the father returned to where his pups still scrapped over the rabbit. He watched the litle foxes for a minute growling and snapping at each other. The male then grabbed Vulpes by the back of his neck and, flipping the little pup over his own back, trotted back up the hill.

The others would learn as a group over the rest of the summer. But tonight Vulpes was going to get a lesson in hunting.

CHAPTER 5

COLINUS
the Quail

 he old fox released his hold from the scruff of Vulpes' neck when they reached the hilltop. The pair then padded along the crest. A three-quarter moon was rising above the treeline in a clear, southwestern sky, and a slight breeze brought some cool relief.

Vulpes imitated nearly everything the old fox did. When his father stopped to test the night wind for scent, Vulpes also sniffed the air. When the old male tracked out a not so fresh rabbit track for a few yards, Vulpes, too, caught the scent, and the hunting instinct swelled inside.

After a while, the father cut into the hardwoods and trotted toward croplands away from the river. He knew of a stubble field, where wheat once grew, between a large cultivated field and a small apple orchard. The wheat stubble was home to many mice and a good spot for a fox pup to learn hunting.

Once in the dry stubble field, the old fox became very quiet. He carefully lifted each foot and placed it down in the brittle wheat stalks. He stopped every few feet and, cocking his head to one side, listened carefully for the telltale rustle of moving mice. Suddenly, he settled back on his haunches, lifted his black-furred front feet and pounced down hard. He had pinned a squealing field mouse between his feet. The old fox grabbed the little rodent in strong teeth and shook it to snap its neck.

Vulpes watched his father with keen interest. The pup started for the mouse, but the old fox growled menacingly. Frightened, Vulpes backed away.

The old male himself gulped down the mouse and then hunted for

another. Twice more he caught mice between his feet and, after killing them in his usual manner, ate them. Vulpes was hungry, too, but each time he started for the kill, he was met by snarls and white fangs.

Then the old fox pushed Vulpes to the front. In time it became clear to the pup that he was to hunt for his own food. He began to step through the field and looked back several times to be sure his father was backing him up.

Vulpes had caught grasshoppers before and once had even captured a small, green frog along the river, but pinning the quick mice was a different matter. Many times, Vulpes heard them scamper before him. But when he pounced, they were not there.

After missing several, Vulpes looked back once more. He watched his father, sitting on his haunches a few feet behind. The old fox had cocked his head again and was listening carefully. Suddenly, he pounced and turned up another mouse.

Vulpes followed the example. Instead of trying to catch the mice as they ran away, the young fox waited patiently for them to move about in the dry wheat stalks. After a moment or so, he could hear the stalks rustle, and on his third leap Vulpes finally caught a mouse.

The old fox trotted over and showed Vulpes how to shake the mouse to snap its neck. He then lay in the stubble field and proudly watched his son devour his first kill.

After the fox pup had caught and eaten another mouse, the old male led him back through the field. He would try to catch something else for the other pups to eat. Mice were fine, but something bigger meant less work and fewer trips home.

Near the river at the end of the stubble field, a mother quail and her brood of nine young slept in a tight bunch among the wheat stalks. This nesting season had been successful for Colinus, the quail. She had laid nine eggs at field's edge in early May. It was unusual that she still had all nine baby quail with her.

During cold, wet springs, nesting quail are sometimes flooded out of the fields or the eggs die from exposure to the cold. On the other hand, a long dry spell, when the chicks are first-born, can cause many to die of thirst. Farmers plowing weed fields or mowing new-grown hay pose a constant threat to nesting quail, too.

The six-week old birds had grown fast. Already three-quarters grown, the young quail were developing feathers on their wings. Soon they would learn flight—their most important means of defense.

Colinus never slept soundly, especially when so many creatures could attack her and her chicks in the night. Owls, skunks, raccoons, foxes, dogs and house cats all prey upon quail at night. In cold weather, Colinus and the other quail slept in a covey, a tight circle, with their heads to the outside of the ring. That way, there was protection in all directions. But now, during the nesting season, the mother quail had to fend for herself and her family.

She was merely dozing when she heard a scraping of wheat stalks. An animal much bigger than a scampering mouse was moving nearby. Colinus cheeped once, quietly, to her sleeping young and slipped away about 20 feet. Whatever the animal was, it was going to pass between her and the nine chicks that huddled silently together.

The old male and his big cross fox pup stalked slowly through the wheat stubble. Vulpes' father pricked up his ears and jerked his head to ground when he caught the hot scent of Colinus. Vulpes also could smell the quail, and it excited him although he did not know why. He had never smelled a quail before.

The wise old fox followed up the hot track quickly. The excitement of the hunt shone in his black, button-like eyes and his lolling red tongue.

Just as he tensed to pounce on Colinus, the smart quail flushed a few feet into the air. Colinus tried an old trick that nesting birds have used for thousands of years. She pretended to have a broken wing and teased the old fox and his stumbling pup into chasing her across the wheat stubble—away from her young.

The pair of foxes were fooled but did not know it. Each time the old male leaped to pin Colinus, the shrewd quail would flutter away a few yards. Finally, when she knew her young were safe, Colinus rocketed away on exploding wings into the night. She swept around the stubble field and landed behind her clutch of frightened chicks. Colinus ran to them and was relieved to find them safe.

Meanwhile, the old fox would have to settle for mice instead of quail to bring to his pups in their riverslope den. Tomorrow night he would take Vulpes and a couple of the other young foxes hunting. The vixen would begin to show some of the others how to hunt, too, and within a week or so, all of the pups would be able to at least catch field mice. That would take away some of the strain of food-providing from the parents.

Colinus gathered her nine young about her and drifted back into fitful bits of sleep. In the morning, she and the chicks would take dew, if there was any, from the grass. If not, and the day was warm again, she would lead them to the river for a drink instead. Then they would spend the day in the wheat stubble, gorging themselves on seeds and small insects.

Many people consider the quail a songbird and not a gamebird. That is one reason that some states have closed seasons on hunting quail. The quail, or bobwhite, as he is often called, is actually both a songbird and a gamebird. The whistle-like **Bob, Bob White** is a wild and thrilling song, familiar in farm fields everywhere.

Quail hunting is big sport, too, especially in the South where the little birds are most abundant. Northern quail often die of exposure and starvation during the cold season. That's a good reason for hunting them. About 90 percent of the quail die each winter anyway. Game biologists believe that this high loss could be turned into sport for hunters and food for the table by allowing limited hunting seasons.

Like the hunting of mourning doves, also a songbird and also a popular gamebird in the South, the shooting of quail will always be a point to argue. Many people will never understand how others can kill quail and why they should. The answer is simple. Like all wild resources that are renewable, be they fish, wildlife, trees or other plants, some must be harvested each year.

Careful cropping of wild things helps make a strong breeding stock for future generations.

Harvesting wild things also makes for steady, balanced populations that the environment can support. Even in northern states, a few quail can be harvested without damaging the bobwhite's survival chances.

Colinus knew nothing of the quail's poor chances of survival. She went on sleeping fitfully.

Cloud cover moved in over Westwind Woods during the dark hours before morning. Dawn came as usual, the blackness giving way to graying half-light and clearer shapes. Agel, the red-winged blackbird, sang loud notes to the new morning from his favorite cattail stalk. Other birds stirred and twittered in a noisy chorus from their leafy roosts throughout Westwind Woods.

Night hunters scurried to their daytime haunts and gave way to the birds of day. Procyon, the raccoon, cracked open one last clam he had fished from the cool river and scampered along the bank, leaving small, hand-like prints in the soft mud on his way to his hollow tree home. Otus, the screech owl, called one last time for his mate who was hunting in the big meadow. Together, the owls flew into the hardwoods where they would sleep out the day.

The rising sun, pushing up above the eastern treeline, was screened behind gathering cloud cover. Westwind Woods would be cooler today, and maybe soon the much-needed rain would come.

Colinus led her nine chicks to the river for a drink and dust bath at first light. The single file troop of quail then returned to the wheat stubble field to pick out a breakfast of seeds and insects.

The mother quail worked her family to the stubble edge next to a small apple orchard. Here she picked at some choice weed seeds that lay scattered throughout the stubble. Some of the chicks followed their mother's example. Others had more fun chasing some slow-moving insects that crawled away into the stubble or clung to blades of grass beneath the apple trees.

The owner of the apple orchard had sprayed his trees for insect control the day before. The poison was working. Many of the invading insects had died and others were dying now. These were the slow-moving ones that lacked the strength to escape from the hungry quail chicks that gobbled them. Several of the chicks gorged themselves on the easy to catch insects.

After a time, Colinus cheeped loudly to gather her brood together for a midmorning nap in the stubble field. The chicks obeyed their mother's calls. Collecting them about her, Colinus led the small band into the stubble field where the quail family napped for several hours.

Meanwhile, the sky grew darker and the wind came up. Soon it blew against the trees, hard, making them dip and moan. A jagged flash of lightning split the disturbed July sky, and loud thunder rolled away up the river and across Westwind Woods.

Colinus listened to the wind and thunder as they grew in force. Fearful of the storm the little quail stirred about her. Their mother decided to seek better shelter and woke her family with quail sounds that were meant for them to follow her.

Four of the chicks did not follow Colinus, though, as she led her troop away. She looked back when she heard them crying. Colinus returned and urged the chicks to follow her at once before the rain came on them hard. But the chicks did not respond. The insect poison gripped them hard, and they trembled with pain and fear.

Colinus was beside herself with fear. She did not know there was nothing to do to save her chicks. She cheeped at them again and again, but all the young quail could do was to follow her a few steps before they stumbled. Soon they grew too weak to stand.

Colinus stayed with her stricken young until the rain came. It began as large, wet drops that spattered the thirsty earth and then swept down in a driving torrent.

Out of a concern for the living young, Colinus tore herself away from her dying chicks. She led the five remaining young quail to better shelter in a dogwood thicket at field's edge. There she huddled the chicks tightly about her.

Colinus did not go back nor did she look back to where the other half of her family lay twitching in the soaking rain.

CHAPTER 6

MARMOTH
the Woodchuck

iolent summer thunderstorms rarely last long. The pelting July rain had stopped long before heat lightning ceased to flash, and booming thunder no longer rolled across Westwind Woods.

The storm broke the midsummer drought that had gripped the land for several days. The Kenawabi River briefly swelled to mud-colored fullness, and a rainbow spanned the western sky just ahead of the sun, peeking to get through the last storm cloud.

The storm had broken the hot spell, too. For the next few weeks, temperatures, for the most part, eased down, and periodic rainfalls washed the green and brown world of Westwind Woods.

These conditions were perfect for growing crops and plantlife, and this helped wild animals greatly. Some of the animals, like the ducks, geese and woodcocks, needed growth and strength for the fall migrations. Others, like the browsing deer, needed to build fat reserves to help them through the winter.

By mid-August, traces of the coming fall were evident. Sunset came moments earlier than it had in July, and sometimes at dusk a trace of coolness was in the air. These temperature changes brought heavy dew to earth where each night it covered the lawns of homes in Riverside Subdivision. At sunrise, dewdrops in the big meadow near the pond glistened like thousands of diamonds to an approving sun that always rose higher for a better look and then succeeded in drying up the splendor.

Most of the new-born animals were nearly full-grown. At first glance, the young woodcocks looked just like their parents except for the slight color

changes in their feathers. The fox pups were hunting as a family each night, and the little foxes were gaining in food-gathering skills. The young sparrow hawks looked just like their colorful parents and could fly nearly as well. Branta still towered over his young, but the five geese were catching up fast and were eager to test their new-grown flight feathers.

One cool morning in the middle of August, Marmoth, the woodchuck, sat upright near his den and looked about him. He could not see the Grayson Road Bridge 300 yards away, but he could hear early morning traffic as cars noisily pounded the old iron span. Maple and oak trees were thick along both sides of the river. Several of the majestic hardwoods, including an odd beech and hickory, were sprinkled around Marmoth's home on a gentle slope that tapered to the river.

Behind the woodchuck's den lay an old pasture where sweet grass grew and where a few black and white Holstein cattle searched it out. Also nearby were other crop fields that belonged to the last farm in Westwind Woods. Marmoth could pick from oats, corn or wheat if he grew tired of munching grass.

Marmoth's mate dozed in the sunlight nearby, and their five young slept and played along the grass-covered slope. Woodchucks have an easy life. They like meadows and grass or grain fields where food is abundant. Woodchucks, or ground hogs as they are sometimes called, have no enemies except man and large predators like wolves, coyotes, bobcats and eagles, none of which lived in Westwind Woods. In winter, when food was scarce and snow-covered, woodchucks simply slept their worries away.

As the sun grew higher and the day grew warmer, Marmoth followed his mate's example and began to doze. Later, he was awakened by the loud roar of a nearby engine and then another. He could hear voices, too, as men hollered to one another.

Marmoth's mate chattered to their young and herded the five woodchucks into the den. Marmoth backed up a few feet nearer the hole and stood high on his hind feet to see what was going on. Some of the Holstein cattle looked up in idle interest at the racket.

The engines died down, coughed and sputtered, and roared again with new life. Marmoth watched as one of the big oaks, marked with blue paint, began to quiver at its leafy top. Then a loud cracking sound spread upriver, and the big tree's grip on life snapped and it crashed to earth. Nearby branches were ripped away, and green oak leaves fluttered down.

The woodcutters had come to Westwind Woods.

With great energy, a small band of men attacked the trees. Their sharp-toothed, yellow chain saws kept up a loud, constant roar as proud oak and maple began toppling, one after another. A third chain saw sputtered and joined the fray.

Other workers, wearing the standard yellow hardhat, began to trim the branches of the felled giants. A dull red bulldozer, its 10-foot wide blade shining in the sunlight, began scooping up the branches in huge piles to be burned later.

A big orange machine, a steam shovel-like monster, with pincers instead of a bucket, worked into the small clearing. Right behind this logging crane someone backed up a flat-bottomed truck with binder chains dragging. The big logs, minus their amputated limbs, would be loaded and shipped off to a mill to make lumber.

Deforestation, or the cutting down of trees, has a tremendous effect on the environment. When carefully managed, though, the cutting of trees can help wildlife by giving them better habitat. Deer, grouse and rabbits, for example, increase much faster in areas where the woods are not heavily covered with mature trees.

The Parks and Recreation Commission's plans to cut the hardwoods, dam the river and create a man-made lake might help some people. Some wildlife, such as the sparrow hawks and the crows and, of course, some of the fish, might not be so directly affected in a bad way. But most of the other animals would suffer greatly, and some would die out.

Forested sections, such as those in Westwind Woods, do more than provide food and shelter for animals. They help to lower stream temperatures. Once the trees are cut, there is no more shade to cool a river—the water heats and fish may die. Trees also help to hold the soil, and without them wasteful erosion results.

Erosion is bad because it puts silt into the rivers, and this can smother the bottom. The bottoms of rivers and lakes are needed to produce food for fish and other animals. Also, gravel sections are used by spawning fish. If silt covers the bottom of a lake or river, neither food production nor spawning can take place.

These same things would happen in Westwind Woods a short time after the big hardwoods were cut. Philo's alder thicket, for example, would be under water once the dam was built, and the woodcock would have to find another nesting site, maybe miles farther north. The deer would have to move on as there would be no protection with the trees gone.

Branta, the goose, could probably find a place to nest along the lakeshore, and the foxes could use their same old den. But the proposed lake would bring swarms of people from Gratiot City, and the pressure would be too great for the wild animals. In the end, most of them would lose.

The cutting of the hardwoods continued all day. After a time, Marmoth grew used to the buzzing saws and the diesel smoke and clanks of heavy duty machines. Several drivers stopped along Grayson Road to watch the yellow-hatted workers and their powerful equipment wrestle with the big trees.

A pair of workers built a large wood-planked sign near the bridge. The white-painted letters showed up well against the brown-stained boards:

Proposed Site of Westwind Lake.
This Land, Donated by Colonel West,
Promises to Provide Recreation
for all area people.
Bellecrest County Parks
and Recreation Commission

A reporter from the Gratiot City daily newspaper took pictures of the sign and toppling trees. He asked questions of some of the workers and spectators and jotted down their answers with a shiny pen in a new notebook.

By late afternoon, nearly an acre of the giant trees had been felled on the east side of the river which was stained with floating green leaves. Small piles of white sawdust dotted the dark ground along with many white-topped stumps. The men and the equipment worked farther upriver as the forest fell away before them.

It was nearly quitting time when a dark blue sedan with two men in the front seat drove up near the bridge. Ray Moore, dressed in jeans and a short-sleeved sweatshirt, sat behind the wheel. Ray looked for a long moment at the bare slope where the woods once stood. Ray shook his head and turned to the man with him.

"They sure don't waste any time, do they, Don?" he said.

Don Reynolds, a middle-aged businessman with tight-cropped hair, agreed. Ray had been keeping him informed ever since the Bellecrest County Board released its plans to allow the Parks and Recreation Commission to build a man-made lake in Westwind Woods. The tall, soft-spoken businessman had an interest in the project. He was president of the Bellecrest County Conservation Club.

"Do you think our club will help seek an injunction?" Ray asked.

"There's no doubt in my mind, Ray," Mr. Reynolds said. "I'm sure our group and others will want to ask the court to put a stop to this. But I'll tell you right now—you better be prepared for a battle. We won't be fighting just a company here, you know. This lake idea is a plan of county government."

"I know," Ray said. "That's why we need all the support we can get."

"Well, you've got ours," Mr. Reynolds said.

The men stepped around the piles of brush and stepped over odd logs and tree stumps as they approached the tree cutters.

"You the foreman?" Ray asked a red-necked, shirtless man with a red bandana about his forehead.

"No, you want the guy over there," the man said with a nod. "Hey, Pete, somebody here to see you."

Pete, the foreman, walked up. He was wearing a white hardhat and a khaki-colored, short-sleeved shirt with a pocket stuffed with papers and a pencil. The unbuttoned front showed a lean, hard frame, and there were sweat stains under the armpits.

"What can I do for you fellows?" he asked.

"We're with a conservation group," Ray offered, "and we'd like to know how many trees you aim to take down."

"All of 'em, of course," the foreman said. "I got a contract with the county board to take down all the trees along the river here. Both sides, up to the markers along the slopes there." He pointed to low hills 200 yards to either side of the river.

A nearby worker choked his chain saw into silence. He and his partner walked up. "Trouble, boss?" he asked.

"Naw, just a couple of guys asking questions," the foreman said.

Other workers gathered around. Ray did not want trouble and was not expecting any. He asked the foreman how far upriver they planned to cut and how long it would take.

"Well, the contract calls for the whole strip to go, all the way upriver, four miles, to those private homes." The foreman did not want any problems either. As a land developer, he had faced these conservation people before. He tried to be pleasant and produced a map of Westwind Woods to show Ray and Mr. Reynolds how deep the lake would be and how much of the tract it would cover.

"How long will the cutting take?" Don asked.

"I'm only working a crew of 10," the foreman said. "I'd say probably most of the fall, by the time we burn off the brush piles and log the timber out."

"You know, we're really against this whole project," Mr. Reynolds announced. "It's going to destroy a lot of natural habitat and wildlife."

"The county board doesn't think so!" the foreman shot back. "Now, if you gentlemen will excuse us, we have some equipment to clean up. It's quitting time. I'm sure you fellows have business to tend to."

Ray looked at his friend. "I guess we do have business to tend to at that," he said.

CHAPTER 7

SYVIL
the Cottontail Rabbit

ore August days passed, the cuttings upriver from Grayson Road Bridge continued. Soon, the yellow-hatted men with their chain saws and diesel equipment had stripped the forest for several hundred yards. The few scattered hickory and beech trees near Marmoth's den on the slope were allowed to stand. Below the slope along the river, though, sawdust piles and hundreds of white-topped stumps marked where the proud trees once stood.

To Steve Nisbet and his friends, August's dwindling days were the subject of much talk. School would begin after Labor Day, and that sad date loomed more closely each day.

Steve's summer had been a happy one. He had spent some time outdoors with his Uncle Ray and had earned some spending money by mowing neighborhood lawns and doing odd jobs. A week's camping up north with other members of Boy Scout Troop 109 was a highlight of his summer.

One evening in late August, Steve and two of the other boys from Riverside Subdivision—Jerry Johnson and Greg Thomas—decided to camp out. The boys loaded their 10-speed bikes with sleeping bags and blankets and stuffed food, cooking utensils, fishing equipment and extra clothes into backpacks.

They planned to ride their bikes on the highway that bordered the eastern edge of Westwind Woods. Turning into the woods at Colonel West's old residence, they would park their 10-speeds at the boarded-up old mansion and hike into the big meadow, a perfect campsite.

The boys had slept in backyards overnight before but had never ventured

on such a two-day trip. It took much coaxing of their worried mothers before permission was granted, along with many stern warnings about being careful.

They left in early morning and by noon had their campsite picked out under a spreading oak next to the big meadow. After setting up their red and white pop tent and gathering enough firewood for the evening's meal, the boys hiked to the river for some afternoon fishing.

"What's that engine racket I hear?" asked Jerry as he added one more leaf worm to the gob already wiggling on his hook.

"Didn't you hear about it?" Steve said. "They're cutting down the woods by Grayson Road."

Jerry shrugged his husky shoulders and cast into the river. "Oh," he said. "What does that mean?"

"Don't you know, dummy?" Greg said. "They're going to flood all this area and make a lake. Pretty soon they'll get these trees, too, right, Steve?"

"That's right," Steve said. "Uncle Ray and some other people are trying to get the cutting stopped."

"So, what's wrong with a lake?" Jerry asked. "Shoot! Got a snag already." Jerry walked a few steps upstream to free his hook. "What's wrong with a lake, anyway?" he repeated. "We'll be able to swim and sail and still fish, too."

Steve remembered something his Uncle Ray had said and offered it as an explanation. "There's nothing wrong with a lake," he said. "It's just that if they build it here, a lot of neat woods will be ruined, and lots of animals driven out of their homes."

Jerry leaned back hard and broke his line, the line parting with a loud snapping sound.

"Sometimes I think you're a nut, Nisbet," he said. "A real nature boy is what you are."

"We couldn't camp out like this if this place was a lake and swarming with people," Steve said.

"That's right," Greg cut in.

"Two nature boys now," Jerry said. "Gimme a hook, Thomas!"

The boys hiked the half-mile back to camp just before dark. Greg carried a stringer of panfish, including two chunky rock bass. That night the boys had a fish supper with pan-fried potatoes and a dessert of marshmallows toasted on sticks by their glowing fire. Then they counted 25 shooting stars before turning in for the night.

As the young campers slept, a quarter moon rose in the eastern sky, and the night sounds of Westwind Woods were in the still air. Somewhere in the marsh, a bullfrog bellowed deeply. The raccoon family splashed in the river shallows as they took turns playing and searching for food.

The meadow was alive with mice rustling through the grass. At the far end, several hundred yards away from the sleeping campers, Odo, the heavy-antlered buck, and his party of a half-dozen whitetail deer browsed. Sleeping nearby in a pocket of grass lined with soft rabbit fur lay a mother cottontail and her two-week old babies.

The five young rabbits slept in a small heap next to the mother who watched over them. Their eyes had been open only a few days, and they still depended upon her for milk and protection. In the middle of the August night, the mother rabbit grew hungry and stole away softly from her sleeping young to nibble some nearby grass.

Sitting on a dead limb atop a towering maple 100 yards away, Bubo, the great horned owl, watched the meadow carefully. Bubo hunted the big meadow often and had caught many mice and a few small mammals during the long summer. His large yellow eyes were well adapted to seeing at night, and he searched the still grass below with a piercing gaze.

Missing little movement below, Bubo spotted the mother rabbit as she poked her head above the grass to listen for danger sounds. Without hesitation, the owl spread his five-foot wide wings and dropped silently from his dead limb perch, which quivered as he left. In the blackness the mother rabbit heard the frightening rush of great wings above her. Not knowing from which direction the attacker came, she cowered in the grass.

She let out a loud death scream as Bubo's sharp, inch-long talons tore into her. Gripping his prize tightly, the night killer carried her away into the blackness.

"What was that?" Jerry hollered, bolting upright in his sleeping bag.

"What was what?" Steve asked, still half-asleep.

"That scream. Some animal just screamed. It sounded like a panther."

"Shut up, Jerry, and go to sleep," Greg said, turning over in his bag.

Jerry lay back down and muttered something about people not believing him. Steve said nothing but lay quietly in his sleeping bag and listened to the night sounds outside. After a while he, too, fell asleep, the cricket music loud in his ears.

The next morning the boys found the five baby rabbits, still huddled together in the fur-lined nest.

"Where do you suppose the mother is?" Greg asked.

"Maybe she got killed last night," Jerry said. "Sure, that's it. I'll bet that scream I heard last night was her getting it from some panther."

"I'm sure, Johnson," Greg said. "There aren't any panthers around here."

"It could have been a fox," Steve said. "Or maybe an owl. There are some pretty big owls around here, too."

The boys left the nest alone but several times during the day went back to check on it. By evening, the boys were packed and ready to go home, but the mother rabbit still had not returned to her nest.

"They're going to die," Steve said. "I know they won't make it through another night. I know Uncle Ray said never to bring home animals from nests, but this is different. Something had to happen to the mother."

He held one of the little rabbits in his hand, a small ball of fur in Steve's palm. The baby cottontail was too weak to stand on its legs. It lay on its side with eyes half-closed.

The boys lined one of their packs with grass and gently laid the rabbits inside, taking care to leave open the top so they could get air.

"We'll split them up when we get home," Greg said.

Once home, Steve told the story to his mother and little sister, Theresa, who petted all the rabbits and wanted to keep one for herself.

"I don't like you bringing animals home, Steve," Ellen Nisbet said. "You know what Uncle Ray says about this."

"But I'm telling you, Mom, this is different," Steve pleaded.

"Well, we'll see what Ray says when he gets home. You go shower now and get ready for bed. I'll warm up supper for you."

After Steve showered and ate supper, the phone rang. It was Jerry.

"I want you to take two rabbits, Steve," he said. "Thomas' ma wouldn't let him have his, and one of mine has already died. They won't eat."

"Did you use an eye-dropper with warm milk like I said?" Steve asked.

"We don't have one," Jerry said. "Listen, Steve, if you don't take these rabbits, they're going to die."

Just then Ray Moore walked in, and Ellen began telling him the story about the rabbits.

"I'll call you back," Steve said.

After hearing the complete story, Ray wasn't really angry about the boys bringing home the rabbits. "I guess you did the right thing," he sighed, "but I doubt if we can save them. Wild animals just don't make it when brought indoors with people."

"We've got to try, Uncle Ray," Steve pleaded. "Can I call Jerry back and get the other two?"

"Well, I suppose," Ray said.

Ray heated milk in a saucepan on the kitchen stove while Steve ran next door. Then, using an eye-dropper, Steve and his uncle began to handfeed the baby cottontails. Two of the rabbits refused to eat, one nibbled at the glass tip of the dropper and a fourth gobbled down the milk greedily.

"I want to name them," Steve said. "What should we name them, Uncle Ray?"

"We're going to be lucky to save even one, Steve. You've got to understand that now."

By morning, two of the cottontails had died, and a third lay quivering on its side. Steve was already by the wooden box where he had placed them the night before when Ray came down from his bedroom to fix morning coffee.

"You're right, Uncle Ray," Steve said. "Only one's going to make it."

"I wouldn't even count on that," Ray shot back. Then, realizing he had hurt his nephew's feelings, he softened. "But if she keeps eating like that, the chances are pretty good," he said.

"I know she'll live. She's got to," Steve promised. "What can I name her?"

Ray looked at his 12-year-old nephew as Steve cradled the baby rabbit gently in his hand and fed it warm milk. The boy's blond hair lay twisted from the night's sleeping, and Steve was slipperless in short, light blue summer pajamas.

"I guess if it was my rabbit, I'd name her Syvil because that's short for the Latin name of the cottontail rabbit," Ray said softly.

"That's a good name," Steve said. "Syvil it is. Thanks, Uncle Ray."

Syvil, the cottontail rabbit, survived, a rare thing Ray kept reminding his nephew. In two weeks' time, the rabbit was nearly half-grown, and under

Ray's direction Steve carried her into the woods and let her be free.

Steve did not complain, and his uncle did not have to tell him that wild animals belong in the wild.

CHAPTER 8

ESOX
the Northern Pike

n young September, the early fall rains came to Westwind Woods. Soon after Labor Day, the skies turned slate gray for several days and rain fell off and on. During this time the yellow-hatted woodcutters were unable to work regularly. They often sat in green company trucks and waited for the order to go home or to go to work. On these wet days in early September the men were usually sent home by 10 a.m.

Rain helped the Kenawabi River to inch back to normal fullness. When the rains finally stopped and the sun returned, Indian summer was in the air. Cool nights were replaced by warmer mornings. The Indian paintbrush with its fiery red-orange flowers spread throughout the meadow. The once green cattails were turning a wheat color, and their dark brown, velvet heads were ripe and full. Algae disappeared from the pond almost overnight, and the farmers drew in their harvest quickly, knowing the warm days would not last forever.

The river ran deep and cool, and sunlight played on its dark surface through spaces in the leaves, now spattered with hints of yellow and orange. Just upriver from the Grayson Road Bridge, the stream switched back sharply and formed a pretzel-shaped oxbow that wound through heavy woods before straightening itself out. The woodcutters with their chainsaws and machinery had not quite reached the sharp turn.

Where the oxbow began, the river formed a deep pool of black pocket water. Here, the current eddied back upstream near a cutaway bank of crumbling earth. This dark pool was about the size of a two-car garage, and

its bottom was covered with marble-sized gravel to a depth of several inches.

Esox, a huge, log-like northern pike, liked this certain hole in the Kenawabi River. He could easily hide from smaller baitfish that entered the pocket and looked for food or shelter. Sometimes other food, such as insects, worms and smaller fish like suckers, chubs and shiners, washed down into the black hole, too.

Deep in this pool, the water was without much current. Esox liked to lie along the bottom, looking much like the many logs, water-soaked and scattered about, and ambush prey. Northern pike are predators, and they will eat nearly anything that fits into their wide, tooth-filled mouths. Esox had eaten young muskrats before, as well as baby ducks and mice and anything else foolish enough to swim through his pool or fall into the river by accident.

On a warm afternoon in mid-September, Esox lay suspended above the bottom a few inches and lazily fanned his fins to remain in place. He watched with cold, hard eyes the clear water above as it swirled in small whirlpools. His dark, weed-like striped body was neatly camouflaged along the brown-black bottom. Esox waited patiently for something to kill.

Later a small school of suckers entered the pool at its lower end, and Esox moved ever so slightly to watch their upstream flight. The foot-long suckers were an excellent meal for the marauding pike whose sleek, snake-like body was wide as a small fence post. As the suckers swam by overhead, Esox suddenly charged upward, the murdering instinct ringing loudly in his pike brain.

Esox chopped up two of the suckers in quick succession and then seized a panic-stricken third fish as it leaped from the water. The other suckers streaked from the pool. While the ripples died and the pool became quiet again, Esox followed up on his kills. He swallowed the suckers, head first, one by one. The pike then settled back to bottom, his deeply hung belly swollen with food.

For Esox, life was easy. When northern pike reach such huge size, they are the masters of other fish. They are never challenged, and they have little problem finding food smaller than they. What Esox did not understand, though, was that his world was constantly threatened by an enemy over which he had no control—man.

Rivers such as the Kenawabi serve many purposes. They not only provide homes and food for wild animals and fish, but are also important to people. Indians and early settlers traveled on America's rivers and built homes and cities near them. Rivers were, and sometimes still are, the lifeblood for people and progress.

Too many times in the past, though, man has paid little attention to taking care of these precious waterways—to use them wisely and not abuse this important natural resource. The result has been widespread pollution and stripping of nearby forests. As the quality of the water goes down, the fish and animals that depend upon water also suffer.

The Kenawabi River flowed through many towns and one large city—Gratiot City—before entering Westwind Woods. There were many chances for pollution from riverside homeowners and factories, and the Kenawabi had been a dirty river in the past.

Keeping a river or lake clean is no easy job. Finding ways to recycle or dump the waste materials is expensive and hard to do. But it is important.

Being a warmwater fish species, Esox did not need the strict conditions of clean water that other fish, such as trout, for example, demand for survival. Still, clean water was important to him, too.

One of the things that can harm fish by changing their reproductive habits is water temperature. Large doses of hot water, dumped into streams by power generating companies, can also harm the development of insects and larvae, upon which many fish species feed. This type of pollution, called thermal pollution, can make a river too warm for some species to thrive in and can cause unwanted weed growth.

Other pollution problems include the dumping of wastes, like sewage, into rivers. These practices were common with both homeowners and large cities. Along rivers like the Kenawabi this seemed to be the cheapest way to get rid of such wastes. This type of pollution is called nontoxic pollution because it is not poisonous.

Sewage from homes and some discharges by factories contains phosphates. A certain amount of phosphates can help the growth of plantlife on a river bottom. Phosphates contain phosphorus, necessary for plant growth. Too many phosphates in a river, though, can cause too much growth and clog a river with weeds.

Although Esox could not remember, the river had been full of sewage discharges and factory spills containing phosphates when he was a young pike. A thin line of dark material—sewage and other nontoxic wastes—once stained the banks as a high water mark. Now, through the efforts of Gratiot City and towns along the Kenawabi, sewer systems and treatment plants handled most of the raw wastes. The Kenawabi River was becoming cleaner each year.

But the threat of another danger—toxic pollution—still remained. Toxic pollution comes from the dumping of poisons—chemical wastes, certain fertilizers and pesticides—into rivers and lakes. Gratiot City was a factory town, and chemicals were used in manufacturing there. Although it was illegal to dump wastes in the rivers, the threat of an accident was always there.

Other pollution problems threatened the Kenawabi River also. For example, only a few months before, a fire at an oil refinery in Gratiot City had burst a huge oil-holding tank. Thick, black crude oil spilled into the river and coated the water for several hundred yards with a dark slick. Some waterfowl were killed since the oil greased their feathers and would not permit them to fly. A few fish died, too. Most of the slick had been contained before it reached Westwind Woods, or more fish and wildlife would have been lost.

Esox had no knowledge of the pollution problems the river had faced and which could come back again. He knew nothing of water quality nor even sensed that his home in the dark, log-studded pool was cleaner than it had ever been before. He only knew that he had stuffed his gullet and was content to lie suspended over the bottom, lazily fanning his fins and digesting the freshly killed suckers. Full or not, though, he would attack nearly anything that entered his lair.

About this time, two fishermen in an aluminum boat drifted downriver and cast brightly colored spoons to dark stretches of water along the shore. Sometimes they would drop a heavy piece of anchor chain into the river and then cast to certain holes for several minutes.

"We're getting close to Grayson Road Bridge," the man in the bow said. "I thought they'd have these woods cut out of here by now."

"Didn't you hear the news last night?" his partner asked. "The Bellecrest County Conservation Club got a court injunction to stop the cutting. They're talking about doing one of those environmental impact studies."

"What do you mean?" the first man asked.

"You know. Someone will have to figure out what this lake project is going to do to the wildlife in the area before they allow the woods to be cut."

"I see," the man in the bow said.

"The conservation club sued the county, and now the judge says that the county has to show why cutting the woods and making a lake is necessary," his partner said.

"Drop the anchor here, Larry," the first man said. "There's a good hole right around this corner."

Larry eased the anchor into the river, and the boat drifted back and forth in the dark current. The fishermen alternated their casts, working the shiny lures through the deep hole.

Far below, Esox saw the glint of sunlight as it flashed across a metal spoon. He pulled up from the deep hole and trailed the slowly wobbling lure. Its flashing brightness interested him, and he closed in fast, a shadowy shape, sinister looking, the age-old joy of attack sweeping through him.

He seized the spoon with strong pike teeth and clamped down hard.

"Look at that fish!" the man in front screamed. "It's huge. A pike—a giant northern pike!"

"Set the hooks hard!" Larry hollered from the stern.

Esox felt the hot sting of the steel in his mouth as the angler rammed his hooks home. He charged once for the surface and quickly boiled the water to a white froth. Esox tried to throw the hooks, but the steel was too deep in his jaw. Fear replaced the murderous thoughts in his brain, and he charged for the river bottom.

"That pike is 20 pounds if he's an ounce!" the man in front shouted, his hands tightly clutching the rod, now bowed in a tight arc. He felt the heavy fish pulsating below and knew the pike was shaking its head to throw the hooks. Line screamed from the reel as Esox tore downstream to the far end of the pool.

"Hold him. Hold him away from that big log," Larry warned. "Don't lose him now. He's as big as an oar! Keep a tight line now, and I'll pull the anchor."

The metal boat drifted downstream. For a minute it looked as though the fish were pulling it. The man in front kept the slack out of his line, and soon the boat pulled up to where the huge pike lay facing the current. A small red and white spoon dangled foolishly from his wide lower jaw.

"Get the net. I'm bringing him in," the man in front said.

"He's still full of vinegar," Larry said. "Give him more time."

"No, I don't think he's hooked that good. Get the net."

Larry dropped the anchor again and then produced the net from under a boat seat. It was a pitifully small net.

"I'll never get all of him in," Larry said, his breath coming in short bursts of excitement. "I'm going to bring it under him and lift him out that way. Keep your line tight and stay out of the way so he doesn't bite us."

The man in front tucked his feet under him and, sitting Buddha-style, peered over the side at the monstrous pike. Esox lay not five feet away, his gills flaring as if in anger, and returned the man's look with a cold stare. The man inched him closer to the boat, and Esox felt the metal net beneath him.

"All right, get ready," Larry said. With a mighty effort, he flung Esox from the water. The pike's belly sagged deeply in the tiny net. His wide fan tail and thick head, as big across as a small garden spade, hung over both ends of the net.

Esox flopped heavily, once, and spilled from the net. The line parted when he crashed to the river in a shower of spray. He quickly sped upstream to his dark lair where he would sulk for many days, unable to eat, and try to work the steel hooks from his mouth.

"I'm sorry, man. I really am sorry," Larry pleaded. "If we only had a bigger net."

"That pike," the man in front said, tears welling up in his eyes, "was the biggest fish I've ever had on."

CHAPTER 9

OTUS

the Screech Owl

ummer had been long in passing for Otus, the screech owl. Thanks to Corvus and the other crows that had smashed their eggs, the adult owls had nothing to do except find food for themselves.

Grasshoppers and other insects, as well as mice and small frogs, were still plentiful in the marsh and meadow, even now in September. Otus had no problem finding enough food to catch and eat.

Dusk often found the 10-inch high owl sitting on a bare hickory limb at meadow's edge. His cat-like face with tufted ears looked like that of his much larger cousin, Bubo, the great horned owl. Otus was no master of the night air, though, as was Bubo. Whenever the smaller screech owl heard Bubo boom loudly, Otus, like the other animals of Westwind Woods, shrank in fear.

Otus and his mate often hunted opposite sides of the meadow and could be heard talking back and forth through the night. Screech owls emit a strange sound—not a hooting or booming noise—but a short, steady rattle unlike anything else in the woods. When graying dawn stained the eastern sky, the chattering pair flew silently into the deeper hardwoods and slept away the day in a hollow tree den.

September is a good fishing month, and many times people in canoes and aluminum boats floated down the river to try their luck. Others hiked into the small pond near the meadow to fish for bluegills and largemouth bass that lived there.

Early one evening shortly after Esox, the northern pike, had his encounter

with the river fishermen, Otus sat on his favorite limb and waited for darkness. When the sun dropped below the trees, his mate began to call to him across the meadow. Otus did not answer her because he was watching something near the pond.

A fisherman and his neighbor stood along the pond edge and studied the surface as it dimpled with feeding bluegills. The men from Bellecrest had visited the pond on early fall evenings in years past. The fisherman set a black plastic pail beside him and began to rig together a flyrod and small surface popper. With any luck, in a half hour or so of serious fishing, he might put a dozen of the slab-sided bluegills into the pail and be on his way home. They would hike the half mile, perhaps with the aid of a flashlight, to Colonel West's old mansion, where the fisherman had parked his car.

Otus watched the intruders with interest. Moments earlier, they had walked right underneath Otus while the screech owl sat rigid on his perch and peered down. The man wore a straw fishing hat, a big-checked, long-sleeve shirt, faded denim jeans and tennis shoes. His friend also wore denim pants and a red flannel shirt. Otus watched as the fisherman tied a popper to the end of his tapered flyline and then false cast a few times over the pond to renew an old feeling for his long rod.

The screech owl was close enough to hear line shoot through the guides and whip back and forth in curls that grew with each wand-like movement the man gave his rod. Soon, the bright red popper touched softly 50 feet away with the barest of ripples. The man waited a moment. He then twitched the rodtip slightly, which made the lure look like a water insect slowly coming to life.

A fat bluegill arrowed for the popper, and the instant his lure was sucked under the man snapped his wrist to set the hook. The bluegill flopped heavily, shattering the glass-like surface of the pond. Feeling an old excitement return, the man held his rod high so the fish would have to work against its strength.

Otus watched as the fishermen played his catch into the shallows. He saw the angler work his popper from the bluegill's mouth and then toss him into the plastic pail. The man smiled to himself and began false casting again to get the proper length in his line.

Not really hungry, Otus put off searching for food and watched as the fisherman enjoyed a half hour of good action. The bluegills came easily and often enough to please the man. The pail by his side began to fill fast with flopping fish.

After a time, the sharp-eyed owl could still see the men, although to the human eye, they appeared as dark, stump-like figures, growing blacker by the minute.

The fisherman's friend lighted a cigarette, and Otus could see its glowing red tip as it rose and fell from his mouth.

Satisfied that he had caught enough fish, the fisherman broke down his flyrod into two sections. His friend flipped the cigarette away, picked up the heavy plastic pail and together they walked across the meadow for home.

By the time the men reached the far end of the meadow, Otus and his mate were calling to each other again. Soon, the owl dropped to the meadow and scooped up a mouse for supper. He flew silently back to the dead limb perch and ripped the mouse apart with his small, sharp beak. After a while, Otus became aware of a bright light near the pond where the man had been fishing. He watched as the red-yellow light grew, spreading wider and higher. Birds of prey do not have a keen sense of smell, but from the direction of the bright light came the odor of smoke. It was a sharp, acrid smell that began to burn his large, sensitive eyes.

Odo, the white-tailed buck, caught the scent of fire, too, from deep in the meadow where he and his small deer herd had been feeding. No rain had fallen for a week or so, and the Indian summer had parched the grass once again. Hungrily, the flames licked through a few marsh cattails. When the fire reached the dried meadow, it really began to take hold. Then, aided by a slight breeze, the fire began to burn furiously.

On an island in the Kenawabi River about a half-mile away a dozen Boy Scouts were camped for the night. The boys, members of Troop 109, were spending the weekend on the river and were trying to earn a merit badge for picking up litter.

All in a row on the wide gravel bar eight shiny aluminum canoe bottoms glinted in the glow of campfire light. Steve and Greg were with the others who all day had been picking up trash along the river. Already that weekend they had filled two spare canoes with bulging green bags full of empty beer cans and other rubbish.

Scoutmaster Bill Verbeck, a college senior, led the boys. Squatting on his knees, he was fueling the main campfire for the last time that night when two Scouts ran to him excitedly.

"Mr. Verbeck, look! A fire across the river!"

The scoutmaster stood up. He looked upriver and could see a bright glow through some scattered trees. His heart began to jump.

"You're right, boys!" he shouted. "It's coming from the big meadow."

Then Mr. Verbeck went into action. He called the boys together and began barking orders like an army drill instructor.

"Ronald, you and Frank get those shovels and rakes by my tent! The rest of you boys grab any shovels, pails and blankets you can find and head for the canoes. Now do what I say and maybe we can get this fire out."

Steve grabbed his olive green Scout flashlight and a pail. Greg balled up the extra blanket they shared in their small pop tent. The boys threw the articles in their canoe and quickly paddled across the river. They and the other boys quickly beached their metal canoes with grating sounds on the silt bar on the other side.

When all were safely across the black river, Mr. Verbeck led them on a run through the few trees between the river and meadow. The party was out of breath when they reached the fire. Once there, Mr. Verbeck quickly sized up the problem.

The fire had already burned an area about the size of two football fields. It had fanned itself into a wide semi-circle of leaping flames that were moving rapidly across the meadow. The curved line of fire was about a block and a half long. Some of the crackling flames were jumping up three feet or more.

Mr. Verbeck knew the fire department could never get into the meadow in time. By the time he could get help from Bellecrest—men and four-wheel drive equipment—the fire would have raged beyond the meadow and into the hardwoods where fire fighters might not contain it. The best idea seemed to be to fight it now. Yet, the young scoutmaster was afraid that his troop members might be hurt if they were not careful.

"All right, listen, you guys," he said between gasps for air. "Do what I say, and nobody will get hurt. We're going to stay together and try to knock it out at its worst—at the far end there where it's about to hit the treeline. Then we'll work back toward the pond." He told the boys with blankets to soak them in the pond, and those with pails were to fill them with water. He organized others with rakes and shovels to beat out the flames.

If the flames had grown much higher and the line of burning grass was much longer, the boys would have had little chance of putting it out. Even so, the little band of 13 fire fighters seemed pretty small, but they attacked the fire like threshers at an outdoor picnic.

Steve had soaked his blanket and he flayed at the fire and tried to smother the hungry flames. Mr. Verbeck had told the boys to save the few precious pails of water to resoak the blankets. The leaping flames quickly dried out Steve's blanket, and once it caught fire. Next to him Bobby Jones, a sixth grade boy that Steve had just met that weekend, struck savagely at the fire with a garden spade.

Smoke burned their lungs and made their eyes water, and the boys began to cough. The hot flames scorched their faces and hands and arms. Steve felt his legs begin to blister beneath their layer of denim, but he did not care. He and the others beat at the fire with a frenzy.

Wild animals have an instinctive fear of fire. Odo and his browsing band had melted back into the forest long before the Boy Scouts arrived. Even though Otus was safe on his hickory perch, he flew down the meadow a hundred yards or so and watched the progress of the fire fighters from there. Mice scampered away before the encroaching flames. Ardea, the great blue heron, left the marsh on silent wings for a safe spot on the river. Meph, the skunk, shuffled away into the yet unburned center of the meadow, and Steve caught a quick glimpse of the black and white animal.

Grass fires do little damage as long as animals and their homes are not destroyed. The grass grows back soon, reclaiming the blackened earth with a fresh blanket of promising green. But fires in woods are another matter. Gray spires of once proud trees stand gaunt above the greening undergrowth for many years. Even though forest fires may be helpful to some animals—like deer and foxes that prefer more open range—they result in an eyesore for a long time. Many years must pass before the last traces go away.

Mr. Verbeck could see that his Scouts were at least checking the fire from spreading into the woods. The scoutmaster cheered his boys along the fire line. They could have been a football team moving the ball ahead to a game-winning touchdown and he might have been their coach.

"We'll whip it now, boys," he encouraged them as he, too, swiped at the flames with a water-soaked blanket.

Mr. Verbeck was right. Troop 109 was winning the battle. They took the rage out of the fire by snuffing out its strength. The once solid red and yellow burning line had been broken into several scattered fires. The boys were now able to tackle these one at a time.

A smoke layer hung low and heavy over the meadow, and gray smoke curled up from blackened ground. In another half hour, only smoke and a few red glowing ashes remained.

When the last flame was put out, Mr. Verbeck called the troop together and formed them into a circle outside the burned area. The boys were exhausted. Many lay flat in the grass and complained of watering eyes and parched throats. Someone passed a bucket of cool water around to drink and splash in hot, sooty faces.

The scoutmaster was proud of his boys and shined a flashlight around the circle at the black streaked faces.

"You guys can't even fight a fire without getting filthy," he teased. "Everybody hits the river for a bath in the morning, but I think a couple of you boys better stay here in case a spark gets it going again."

"Steve and I will," Greg Thomas offered.

"You're on," Mr. Verbeck said. "That hooty owl I hear can keep you company." Otus' mate once again called to him in the still night.

"How did the fire get started, Mr. Verbeck?" someone asked.

"Oh, I suppose someone left a campfire going or tossed a match or smoke away without crushing it," Mr. Verbeck said.

"I'm going to be too tired to pick up junk again tomorrow," another boy said.

"Don't worry about that," Mr. Verbeck said proudly. "I think you guys have earned more than one merit badge this weekend."

CHAPTER 10

TAXUS
the Badger

he next morning's sun was barely an hour old when Steve and Greg wandered back to camp. Luckily, the fire had not flared up again during the night, and now in full light the boys could survey the damage. About five acres of meadow was charred. Back at camp, the other boys were already swimming in the river and some rubbed themselves into a soapy lather and washed away the grime of last night's battle.

On this cool September morning, fog curled like camp smoke from the cool, dark river. Steve did not feel like stripping down and plunging in.

He had never felt dirtier in his life. His eyes were puffy and still smarted, and his grimy face was streaked with tears. The hair on his aching arms was singed in a couple of places, too. The other boys had looked no better, and Steve knew he should get into the water. To go home filthy was to risk a scolding and to threaten further chances at camping.

"You're it for tag, Steve," a boy said as he reached up over the side of the canoe and slapped Steve on the arm.

After cleaning up in the river, the boys ate a breakfast of scrambled eggs, potato pancakes, apple juice and cocoa. By 10:30, they had loaded the canoes and were drifting downstream.

Scoutmaster Verbeck had picked the big island for a campsite. It was deep in the Westwind Woods tract and made a perfect half-way stop for a two-day float trip. The island was a couple hundred yards long and about 50 yards wide at its widest point and was covered with scattered brush and

poplar trees. Firewood was everywhere, and the gravel bar made a perfect spot to beach canoes at night.

It has been Mr. Verbeck's idea to run the river on a litter pickup. As far as he knew, no one had ever done this, and it seemed like a perfect project for his Boy Scouts.

Mr. Verbeck had floated the Kenawabi a couple of weeks before and then knew that his fears about the river being heavily littered were right. People had mostly thrown away beer and pop cans. Also, the Scouts were turning up many other interesting items like old tires, shoes, scrap metal, a wooden chest full of water-soaked rags, a seat from an automobile and so on. Much of the debris probably had come from Gratiot City as well as from the village of Bellecrest where careless people threw their junk into the river from bridges and from the bank.

Much of the trash was partly hidden by lush September forest growth. Most of it lay scattered along the banks, deposited there by high water in the spring.

The scoutmaster had made arrangements with the mayor's office to have a garbage truck from the village meet them at Grayson Road Bridge. The editor of the weekly paper promised to take pictures of the Scouts and their collection of junk. He said he would write an editorial criticizing those who littered.

Littering has become a huge problem in this country because many people have developed a throwaway habit. A research study Mr. Verbeck had read for one of his college classes had helped interest him in this topic. The report showed that citizens who litter are often those with the most money. Throwing things away was a symbol of their spending power.

One of the ways to whip the litter problem was to educate people against it. Another was to provide barrels and other containers for people to throw away their junk. Even with these efforts, though, the littering problem has not disappeared. Each year it becomes more costly to pick up as well as unsightly to look at.

In recent years, American packaging and container companies have done a big business in making more and more throwaway bottles and cans. Most people like the convenience of being able to toss things away when they are finished with them. They seem willing to pay a higher cost for this privilege. But much wasted energy goes into making containers which are never used again except for the few that are sometimes collected and recycled. Most of the throwaways have to be stored in landfill dumps, and many of these are bursting with fullness across the country.

Mr. Verbeck had explained these things to the Scouts and asked them how they thought the river could best be picked up. The boys suggested that they work in three two-man teams with six boys to each side. Two boys would comb the river banks with rakes to pull trash together. The other four would hold together a small band of four lashed canoes. The system was working well, and the boys were filling their canoes fast with bulging green garbage bags. Every half mile or so, the boys would switch positions. It was turning into quite a busy weekend for Troop 109 what with camping, fighting a fire and picking up litter.

Besides being an eyesore and costly to clean up, littering also poses a real danger to wildlife. Geese and ducks have been known to swallow the ring pull tabs on canned pop and beer and choke to death as a result. The plastic throwaway six-pack holders also are dangerous. Sometimes fish, as well as birds and muskrats get stuck in the holes as they pick them up around their heads and bodies while swimming.

Most throwaway items do not break down in the environment. They remain there until picked up, sometimes years later. Examples of the worst materials are glass, metal, plastics and nylon. Sometimes the materials do break down and cause even bigger problems since a poison may be formed. The backing on certain photographic film, for example, goes through a chemical breakdown and can kill animals that come in contact with it.

Mr. Verbeck was especially proud of his Scouts when he overheard many of their comments about littering.

"Wow, who'd be stupid enough to throw this away?" was a typical statement. Others were, "These people ought to be fined or made to come out here and pick up their junk," and "Look at all this trash. If people only knew how much stuff they throw away."

While the boys scoured the riverbanks for rubbish, a strange looking animal slid down a riverbank slope a couple of curves downstream. The animal was steel gray in color with bits of brown fur streaked along its sides and back and a mask-like face of white and brown bars.

Taxus, the badger, was the only one of her kind in Westwind Woods. A shy animal, badgers are rarely seen.

Bigger than a large raccoon, Taxus was built low to the ground and was nearly as wide as she was long. Her powerful stubby legs propelled her along very rapidly for such a bulky animal. When cornered, badgers are dangerous to people and dogs and have been known to fight to the death. A member of the skunk family, badgers have strong, sharp teeth and long, razor-sharp claws that aid them in digging and in defense.

Taxus' home was a large den on a hardwood slope. It was located between the old fox den and Marmoth, the woodchuck's home near the bridge except that Taxus' den was across the river in the hardwoods.

Taxus had been seen by only a handful of human beings in her long life of 14 years. Badgers have been known to live 20 years or more. She and her mate had raised several litters over the years, and the young ones had all moved on to other areas.

Since her mate had been killed by a car on the highway several years ago, Taxus had not raised any new families. In Westwind Woods, at least, Taxus, along with Ardea, the great blue heron, was an endangered species.

An endangered species is an animal or bird that is almost extinct.

Her mate's death on the highway was not unusual. Each year, many thousands of deer, raccoons, porcupines, opossums, squirrels, rabbits and other animals are killed on American roads. Many times, these accidents can't be helped, especially at night when some animals stand right in the road and stare into car lights. Highway deaths are just one of the prices wild animals pay when their habitat and human habitat come together.

It was now early afternoon, and the day had warmed. Being a night hunter of small mammals and insects, Taxus had been sleeping in her den when she awoke very thirsty. She had ambled to the river and now shuffled across a sand bar to get a drink from the river.

The boys had seen much wildlife on the river so far that weekend. Kingfishers had chattered at them on every bend, it seemed. They had watched hawks and crows, a pair of wood ducks and several mallards. One of the canoes in front startled Branta and his small band of Canada geese into flight. But none of the boys, or even Mr. Verbeck for that matter, had ever seen a badger.

Steve and Greg were in one of the lead canoes and had a good look at the strange animal on the sandbar.

"Mr. Verbeck, look!" Greg said excitedly. "What is that animal?"

Taxus threw up her head and looked intently at the approaching canoes.

"Well, I don't know for sure," Mr. Verbeck said hesitating. "It looks something like a raccoon, but I—wait a minute. I'll bet it's a badger. Sure, it's got to be a badger, but I didn't know any lived around here."

Taxus took a long look at the canoes filled with green plastic bags and Boy Scouts. Then she scampered up the hill, her heavy, wide flanks rippling as she scaled the bank.

"Boys, that's really rare to see a badger," the scoutmaster said. "I'll bet it has a den up there in the woods somewhere."

Steve thought about the badger during the afternoon. When the canoes reached the cutover area upstream from Grayson Road Bridge, he was glad the court had made the woodcutters stop taking down the trees. Waiting at the bridge was a yellow garbage truck. As the canoes pulled into shore, Steve wondered what would happen to the animals of Westwind Woods if all the trees were taken out.

"I really hope the court stops these lumberjacks for good," Steve said to his friend Greg while they threw their bags of litter into the garbage truck.

CHAPTER 11

PHAS
the Ring-Necked Pheasant

s September edged into October, Westwind Woods donned a new look. Greens and browns were hard to find in the hardwoods where oranges, reds and yellows now rioted in October sunlight. Nature's paintbrush dabbled with the smallest oak and maple and turned the drabbest leaves into works of art.

Thin shell ice ringed the pond on the chilly autumn mornings, and heavy dew often appeared as frost on car windows. Steve and the other students who waited for the school bus to pick them up in Riverside Subdivision wore jackets and sweaters by mid-October. They could see each other's breath as they chatted about the day's events.

The blazing colors and drop in temperatures were not the only changes occurring in Westwind Woods. Ondrata, the muskrat, had grown a new coat of dark, thick fur for winter. Odo and the other deer had changed from rusty browns to a gunsmoke gray that would soon blend well with winter's naked hardwoods.

Philo and her woodcock family had pushed south two weeks ago, returning to their wintering grounds in Louisiana. Branta and his family of Canada geese had drifted south a hundred miles to a sprawling national waterfowl refuge. Other geese gathered here, too, and soon would leave the state in long V-shaped lines for a warmer climate.

Except for Farmer Greene, most of the farmers had gathered their crops. Farmer Greene was usually the last to draw his harvest, and he seemed to do so with reluctance each year. He liked to see the ripe fields of oats, corn and soybeans, and he knew that to cut them down was to deprive wildlife of

some of their food. October would soon be easing into November, though, and Farmer Greene knew he would have to get the balance of his crops in soon.

Early one glorious October morning, a colorful cock pheasant led a small troop of brown hens and younger roosters into Farmer Greene's big cornfield. The pheasants had been roosting in a small piece of high pasture grass nearby the ripe corn. Every day at first light, they marched single file, with Phas, the big, gaudy ring-necked pheasant, up front into the corn for breakfast.

Phas was a two-year-old bird that had sired many chicks last spring, some of which were with him now. He had survived his first hunting season and last year's snow and ice storms.

Pheasants were once widespread throughout the Midwest and Great Plains states, such as South Dakota and Nebraska, but in recent years their numbers had fallen off. Predators and rough winters account for some of the annual losses. A bigger reason, though, for their decline is the practice of cleanpicking crops, which leaves little food behind for wildlife. Other reasons are shrinking habitat, poisonous sprays and mowing of hayfields when hens are on the eggs.

Hunting does little to change pheasant populations from year to year. Pheasants can lose 50 percent of their numbers by spring anyway, and game biologists see no harm whatever in controlled hunting seasons.

Autumn brings out bright colors in gamebirds, and Phas was no exception. As he led his harem into the cornfield, he strutted, showing off his brilliant breast feathers of rust-red with green tips. The white ring about his neck was a royal collar that set off a shining dark green head, yellow beak, bright eye patches of crimson and a light brown crown and feather tufts of green again.

Phas was not a true American gamebird. In 1881, his ancestors had been imported from China, where many colorful and exotic birds live. The Chinese or ring-necked pheasant had adapted well to its new American home. In a few years, pheasants were well enough established to allow a hunting season in some states. The introduction of this great gamebird had been very successful.

Success is not always the result, though, when foreign birds and animals are stocked somewhere else. When carp were brought to American ponds and lakes from Europe, many people thought they would be a great addition to native gamefish. Instead, carp have multiplied so rapidly that they dominate many warmwater lakes and streams in this country. These big, sluggish fish dirty the water and sometimes ruin the spawning sites of more important warmwater species, like northern pike, bass and bluegills. American streams and lakes would be much better off if the carp had stayed in Europe.

On the other hand, nobody would argue that the brown trout should never have been brought to the United States. These great gamefish also were introduced from Europe and are now found in swift rivers and cold lakes across the country. Browns have become one of our most sought after fish and are proof that foreign species can also do well here.

The problem is that no one knows for sure just what will happen when strange animals and birds are planted somewhere else. Brown trout and Chinese pheasants are positive examples; carp are not. Other problem birds like sparrows and starlings were brought here from England a century or so ago. Starlings sometimes flock together by the millions and damage the landscape. They also may pose a health hazard when they concentrate so thickly.

Although Phas was not a native American gamebird, over the years his species had come to be accepted as such. Phas had no knowledge of this. The crop fields and swales of Westwind Woods were as much a home to him as they were to Vulpes, the cross fox, or Marmoth, the woodchuck, or any other native animal.

Another thing that Phas did not know was that today was the first day of the small game hunting season in this part of the state. That meant that he and the other male pheasants, as well as rabbits and squirrels, would be legal targets for the next few weeks.

To the hungry pheasants, this mid-October morning was just like any other autumn day, and as usual the pheasants had breakfast on their minds. A slight breeze rustled the paper leaves of the cornstalks. Phas and the others fanned out along the rows, deep into the golden brown corn, until they found knocked-down stalks that held a plump ear or two of ripe field corn.

Such golden fall days are lazy ones for pheasants. Grasshoppers still career across weed fields and ripening wild fruit such as dogwood berries and grapes are everywhere, as are weed seeds and cultivated grains. Fall and its abundance of food make for an outdoor grocery store. Wild animals never have it so good at any other time of year, and the reason is simple. Autumn is the time for animals to grow strong and build fat reserves against the leaner, colder days of winter when snow, ice and freezing temperatures often lock up the land in a white deepfreeze and make food hard to find.

The October sunlight bathed Westwind Woods in a golden glow this day. His hunger satisfied and his food crop bulging with corn, Phas began to lead the others back to the high pasture grass. Here they would nap in the warm sun. Later, in the middle of the afternoon, the pheasants would stroll back to the cornfield for another feast. As he was leaving the rows of corn, Phas heard the distant barking of a dog. The steady chop of the animal's deep voice carried far in the autumn stillness.

Phas paused and listened to the dog's music. Something popped into the pheasant's brain that he had experienced this before, but he could not pinpoint the details or their meaning. Suddenly, a second dog broke into a full-throated bawl close by. Now Phas knew—hunters were here!

They were close by, and their dogs had picked up the pheasants' scent on the still moist ground. Phas and the others scooted down the last couple of corn rows and rushed into the pasture land. The cock pheasant heard men's voices as they urged their dogs on. All of this commotion seemed frighteningly close.

On one side at the end of the pasture land, a freshly tilled field lay bare. Some of the hens and younger roosters foolishly sprinted in that direction. Phas was smart and instead moved toward the other side of the pasture where he knew woods grew thick and safe. He and a couple of hens that followed him might escape in the tangle of trees.

He heard the excited cackling of one of the other birds as the young rooster burst from cover. There had been no place to run except onto the open field, and the juvenile cock pheasant had crouched in the edge cover until the last possible moment. A loud crashing boom followed, and someone hollered, "I got him, Dad." Then more cackling and more shots.

One of the bellowing dogs followed Phas' hot track into the woods. When the black and white mongrel closed in fast, Phas burst in a blaze of color from some oak saplings. The hunters did not see Phas or the hens explode on swift wings and could not have gotten off a decent shot even if they had. If he used his wits, Phas would survive yet another hunting season. The first day is usually the toughest since after that many hunters case their guns for another year.

Phas and the hens flew a hundred yards through the woods and then curved back toward the fields. They aimed for a soybean field yet unpicked and hit the ground running.

Working the center of a nearby stubble field were another hunter and his liver-colored German short-haired pointer. The hunter had seen Phas land in the soybeans. Although Farmer Greene had given him permission to hunt, he had asked that the man stay out of his soybeans. But the man wanted the big rooster very badly. Without hesitation, he whistled to his dog and pushed into the soybeans.

The man was a game violator and over the years had broken the laws, including the killing of hen pheasants, many times. Even he didn't know why he cheated at the sports of hunting and fishing that he enjoyed so much. Perhaps it was the thrill of doing something wrong and maybe getting away with it. Or maybe he had no respect for laws and authority. He did not know nor did he care to wonder about it. Violating was something in his blood that could not be explained.

Right away his sharp-nosed pointer picked up Phas' smoking track. The wise rooster already knew that he was being pursued again. His keen sense of hearing picked up the scraping noise of weeds against the hunter's new canvas pants, and now he heard the man loudly rack a shell into his shotgun chamber.

Phas ran hard along the soybean rows for a couple hundred yards. When he knew he had outdistanced the hunter and his dog for the moment, he flushed low from the soybeans and glided just above them for a long way and then dropped down again. This tactic was something he had learned late in the season last year, and it had saved his life once again today.

The man saw the big rooster get away, and he swore softly to himself. He wanted that cock pheasant badly because he knew the bird was older and bigger than most, but he also knew he would never get him up again today. He swore again, loudly, and spat in the soybeans.

Just then his short-haired pointer went stiff with attention. "Probably one of the hens," the man said aloud. "Take her, Spike." The eager pointer rushed ahead and swept a drab hen, quite a contrast to the colorful Phas, from the soybeans.

The man did not hesitate as he pulled his gun up. He blotted out the brown target and squeezed off a shot. A loud crash followed, and the hen crumpled to earth. The man felt no excitement over his act. He routinely walked over to the downed bird and again, without feeling, picked her up and stuffed her into his game pouch. His only regret was that the hen was not the gaudy rooster he wanted so badly.

"Mister, I'd like to see your license and gun, please," he heard a voice behind him say.

The game violator spun around and stood face to face with a conservation officer.

"I saw you shoot that hen on purpose," the law officer in dark green pants and a beige shirt said. "Give me your gun."

"It was a mistake, Officer," the man pleaded. "I thought I heard it cackle and figured it was a rooster."

"No way," the officer said. "If I'm to believe that, then you're not only color blind but blind and deaf as well. Are you sure that dog of yours isn't the seeing-eye type? Now give me the gun."

The violator handed over his weapon. "What will happen to me?" he asked, fear rising in his voice.

"Mister, that's up to the judge. You'll find out soon enough."

"Can't you give me a break?" he asked.

"Leash up your dog and let's go," the officer said abruptly. "You're all done hunting for a long time."

CHAPTER 12

SCIURUS

the Fox Squirrel

ciurus, the fox squirrel, popped his head up and listened carefully. Stretched out along an upper oak tree limb, he had been napping in the warm afternoon sun. The snap of a twig, a definite danger noise, had jerked him from sleep.

Suspicious, he looked about him through the pale orange oak leaves, curled with October frost, to the forest floor below. In the stillness of this golden afternoon, Sciurus heard the slow crackling of patient footsteps in new leaves that layered the earth.

The fox squirrel chattered loudly to warn his mate and the other squirrels in nearby trees. An intruder, quite possibly a hunter, had entered their woodlot.

In another moment, Sciurus could see him, an old man who stepped carefully among the hardwood saplings as he approached the giant oaks where the squirrels made their nests. He was a hunter all right, although Scirius could not have known that. The man wore leather boots, brown canvas pants and a large, bulky parka, painted with a pattern of dead leaves. His brown camouflage blended well with the dying glory of these frost-fired October woods.

Sciurus flattened himself along the rough bark of the limb and listened as the man passed underneath. The hunter's footsteps crackled the brittle leaves like breakfast cereal. This was not the first time that hunters had interrupted Sciurus' mellow, autumn days. The one-acre woodlot in Farmer Greene's fields, the same grove where Falco, the sparrow hawk, nested, was popular with squirrel hunters. The tall oaks and iron-gray beech trees

were home to several families of fox squirrels. They found the supply of nuts and abundance of grain fields much to their liking.

The old, gray-haired hunter moved to Sciurus' oak and stopped. He had heard the squirrel's chatter and decided to squat on the ground with his back against the shaggy black trunk. Cradling a shiny barreled shotgun across his knees, the man knew he would have a wait of a half hour or so before the squirrels would stir again.

A retired farmer who for many years had worked the land next to Farmer Greene, the old man enjoyed hunting squirrels. He hunted the woods many times each fall in the early mornings and late afternoons. Squirrels are most active then, and the chances of bagging a bushytail are good at those times. Several million squirrels are harvested each year across the U.S., and they are as popular with hunters as are cottontail rabbits.

The man was a good hunter, and he liked to pit his patience and knowledge against that of the squirrels. He never fired shotgun blasts into the balls of leaves where the squirrels nested and slept at night as he had known others to do. This practice often kills the squirrels, which cannot be claimed, and is a waste. The man did not believe in wasting game. He had told this to his son many times and more recently to his grandson.

His hike into the woods having warmed him, the old man tilted back his brown hunting cap and zipped open the heavy parka. The warm October sun rays felt pleasant on his weather-lined face, and he was happy to be here at this moment in the woods alone. Soon, his head began to droop, and once or twice he caught himself drowsing off to sleep. "Might as well catch a few minutes' shut-eye," he thought to himself. "Squirrels won't show for a time, anyway."

In another moment, he relaxed his grip on the shotgun and lolled his head to shoulder as sleep overtook him. Soon, the peaceful old man began to take measured breaths through a sagged open mouth.

High above in the oak tree, Sciurus had not fallen back asleep. He knew from experience that he must be patient if he wanted to stay alive. He stayed flattened out on the tree limb for more than a quarter hour. Finally, he thought it might be safe to at least stir a little and check the area out for danger. He sat back on his haunches, his tail plume drooping several inches below the branch. Everything seemed all right. Scirius then inched toward the massive trunk and upon reaching it, circled the tree a couple of times.

He saw the silent hulk of the hunter against the tree far below. Sciurus studied it for a long moment and decided that it posed no danger. The afternoon was wasting fast, and Sciurus wanted to store a few more acorns away for winter before darkness came. He dashed to a limb several feet above and then ventured out to its spindly end where bunches of acorns grew.

The mast crop was heavy this fall. Already Sciurus and the other squirrels had spent many days stuffing themselves with the acorns and burying many more in the ground. Most of those acorns they would never find when snow lay like a white blanket over the frozen ground. Deer and mice and maybe a few pheasants might unearth some of the acorns, too, but most would lie in the ground until spring. Then a lucky few would take root in the moist earth and start new oak trees. Some of the bigger oaks had several dozen oak saplings and smaller shoots clustered about their trunks like an old woman with a throng of attentive grandchildren.

Sciurus knew nothing of his importance as a planter of forests. It was simple instinct that moved him to bite the acorns free and send them crashing to the leaf-strewn floor below. Several bounced near the sleeping hunter. It wasn't until one small bunch hit him in the head that the old man finally came alive.

"What's going on?" he sputtered and jerked himself to his feet. He knew instantly what had happened and quickly scanned the treetops above for any sign of squirrel movement. Sciurus, meanwhile, had seen the old hunter leap to his feet. Frightened, he zipped around the back of the tree to hide.

The old man saw a flash of red-brown fur and knew the fox squirrel was hiding on the back side of the oak. After a moment, he bent down and picked up the acorn clump and then tossed it to the other side of the tree. Startled again, Sciurus ducked around to the front of the tree, and the old man took a hasty shot at him.

A loud crash ripped through the hardwood grove, and oak bark splintered from the tree. "Missed him!" the old man said in surprise. "How could I have missed him?"

In a panic, Sciurus raced to the tree top and plunged into a thick patch of leaves. Here he wedged himself as a tight ball against a fork in the tree and trembled. The old man searched the upper branches for a long moment but could not see the hidden squirrel. He then picked up his empty red shell and sniffed the pungent odor of gunsmoke. He stuffed the burned hull into his canvas pants pocket. "Won't nothin' move in these woods now 'till dark," he muttered to himself. "Might as well head home for supper. Don't want to miss the town meeting tonight, anyhow."

Gray twilight thickened over the fields and woods as the old man shuffled home, softly whistling snatches of a forgotten song. Approaching his battered, old barn, he saw the dim glow of a low-burning light in the window of their farm home. He was hungry and knew his wife would have a supper of hot biscuits and beef stew waiting for him. It had been a good afternoon in the woods. The fact that his game pouch did not bulge with fox squirrels was not important.

As the dusk gathered, Sciurus found enough courage to leave his high perch. He sneaked along an upper limb until he found an acorn bunch. He ate quickly and then scampered to his nest of leaves where he would sleep.

Later that evening, a large crowd of people gathered at the old township hall in Bellecrest village. The meeting had been planned by the mayor of Bellecrest and the County Board of Commissioners to explain their plans for Westwind Woods to be turned into a lake. Someone from the Department of Natural Resources would be there to answer questions about the Environmental Impact Study ordered by the court. The meeting would also give citizens a chance to express their feelings on the subject.

Mr. Reynolds, Ray and other conservation club members welcomed the chance to explain why they felt that destroying the woods would damage the environment. They hoped to convince others, but they also knew that these meetings are usually emotion-charged. Quite often, people have their minds made up long before.

A pair of sheriff's deputies began turning away the crowd 15 minutes before the 8 p.m. meeting time. The white, clapboard building, used years before as a one-room schoolhouse, was jammed with citizens, government people and reporters. A camera crew from the television station in Gratiot City jockeyed for position in the cramped building.

Seated in front with several others at a long table, Mayor Burns pounded the group to silence with his wooden gavel. He then explained the meeting's purpose. Mayor Burns said that the chairman of the County Board of Commissioners would give a brief talk. He would be followed by a speaker from the DNR, and then citizens could have the microphone for three minutes each to express their views.

Mayor Burns sat down, and John Dunlop, a short, balding man in his forties, took his place at the lectern. After introducing himself as chairman of the county board, he produced a large chart of Westwind Woods. Mr. Dunlop began to tell the audience about the county's original plans for a lake. While the bright television lights glared in the crowded room, he showed where a beach for swimming would be built. He then pointed out bath houses, boat ramps, picnic grounds and how a sailing area was planned. A few people clapped to show their appreciation for the idea, but grew quiet again when Mayor Burns threatened with his gavel.

"But, apparently, we were wrong," Mr. Dunlop said, "and now we're being sued for having the woods cut. We're being told that we should not have allowed the Parks and Recreation Commission to make a lake without first consulting you, the people of Bellecrest County."

Several other people began to clap and cheer in agreement. Mayor Burns rapped sharply several times with his wooden gavel.

"I know this is an emotional issue," he bellowed, "but I'm determined to keep order here! Everyone will have a chance to speak his mind, but we're going to have order in this room!"

The outburst stopped, and Mr. Dunlop continued, "So when the conservation club filed its suit against the county, Judge Garver issued a temporary order to stop the cutting until an Environmental Impact Study could be conducted. We're waiting the results of that now."

He was replaced at the lectern by the DNR speaker. This new speaker explained that a team of five fish and wildlife biologists were studying Westwind Woods at this time. Several people asked what they were finding out, but the speaker, a tall man who looked like a lawyer with his brown leather briefcase, wire-rimmed glasses and neatly pressed business suit, would not comment. "The results will be released to Judge Garver along with our suggestions," he said.

Ray Moore rose from the crowd. After being recognized by Mayor Burns, he asked the DNR official, "Do you mean that if your report shows that some animals might lose their homes and be destroyed, then your suggestion would be to scrap the lake idea?"

"I didn't say that," the man replied. "We might advise the county parks people to adjust their plan according to our findings, but that does not mean that the lake would have to be scrapped.''

A look of disgust spread across Ray's face. "That's what I thought," he said and sat down.

An hour passed, and no one had left the packed room, which was now becoming warm even though the October night outside, where several people still milled about, was cool.

Mayor Burns turned the meeting over to citizens with something to say. He allowed each speaker three minutes and on several occasions had to quiet the noisy crowd with repeated whacks of his wooden gavel.

Pete, the foreman of the woodcutters, stirred the crowd the most when he threatened to sue the county if he was not allowed to finish cutting the trees. He waved a copy of his contract before them and bitterly reminded everyone that he was being cheated from earning his living.

"Every day we don't cut timber costs me down time in men and equipment," he shouted. "If my company has to pay out much more in unemployment, we'll go belly up by Christmas. If you people didn't want a lake here, you should have told us before hiring us to cut the woods down!"

The anger flashed in his red face and loud voice, and he stomped across the wooden floor to his seat in the crowd.

Others spoke up, too. A farmer was upset because he felt that hordes of people would spill out of the proposed park into his crop fields, break down his fences and molest his livestock. On the other hand, several merchants in a row talked about the business and tax rewards that would come if the lake were built.

They were followed by a spokeswoman from the recreation department of Gratiot City. "City folks, as well as country people, will appreciate Westwind Lake," she said, "and I don't have to remind you of the need the whole county has right now for public recreation."

Don Reynolds, Ray Moore and the other conservation people listened carefully to the parade of speakers who talked in favor of the lake project.

"We better try to swing this back the other way," Mr. Reynolds said. "I think it's time I said a few things."

CHAPTER 13

SPONSA
the Wood Duck

r. Reynolds walked through the crowded township hall to the lectern that faced the audience. He felt a little nervous, as he always was before speaking to a large group. Yet he was never as sure of himself or his beliefs as he felt right now.

He looked over the blur of faces and remembered that he had only three minutes. "Three minutes," he thought to himself, "to explain something to people that they should know and feel in their hearts." Then his thoughts became words, and he began to say similar things to the crowd.

"I can't begin to explain to you in three minutes," Mr. Reynolds said, "something as complicated as man's relationship to nature, but I'm going to try. My name is Don Reynolds, and I'm president of the Bellecrest County Conservation Club."

The tall, soft-spoken man with the closely cropped hair reminded the audience that it was his group that had sued the county. He said the county's lake proposal had moved too fast. He felt that the people's opinions should have been asked first. "Not enough consideration has gone into the lake plan and its effects on wildlife," he said, "and so the conservation club forced a halt to the cutting."

He said that public recreation was a good thing but not at the expense of destroying habitat so rich in natural resources. "I doubt if many of you realize the richness of Westwind Woods," Mr. Reynolds said, "or the many game animals and other wild creatures that live there."

An undertone of conversation began to buzz throughout the room. He went on, "If public recreation is what you want, then why not combine it

with an educational project? We could turn Westwind Woods into one of the finest nature preserves in the state, or maybe even the country, for that matter. People could still come and enjoy the land and see the wild things in their natural habitat."

"And just how much would that rip us in taxes?" someone hollered across the room.

"Certainly not as much as it costs to rip down all the woods and build a man-made lake," Mr. Reynolds said. He paused for a moment.

"I think the people will finally decide what becomes of Westwind Woods," Mr. Reynolds went on. "But I think all the facts need to be brought together first. Why wasn't an EIS done earlier, for example? Why didn't the county consider other sites for the lake? And most importantly, why weren't you and I asked how we felt before the cutting began?

"The conservation clubs have always stood firm against destroying natural habitat, no matter what the purpose. Building a dam for electricity or draining a marsh for a shopping center or ruining a tremendous natural resource like Westwind Woods to build a lake are all wrong if the environment must suffer greatly for it."

Again, conversation began to spread in the tiny room. "I see my time is about up," Mr. Reynolds said, "so let me just say that we feel the EIS will prove us right and that most of you will see that we are right." He looked at Pete, foreman of the woodcutters, and said, "I know what it's like to lose work, and maybe you should be paid for your loss. But I hope you and others can put personal profit aside and do what is best for the land and the people." Mr. Reynolds then returned to his seat next to Ray.

The next speaker, a store owner from Bellecrest, began, "When I say that the lake is a good idea, I'm thinking, as Mr. Reynolds just suggested, of the land and the people..."

"What do you think?" Mr. Reynolds whispered to Ray.

"Well, I believe you got a few heads to thinking hard, and you may have won a few people to our cause."

"Maybe, maybe not," Mr. Reynolds replied. "But we sure have our work cut out for us, Ray. These people seem to be for the lake."

Bellecrest village hummed with news of the town meeting for several days. People began to wonder just what the DNR survey would show and what the County Board of Commissioners would do when they received the report in another month or so.

Meanwhile, the animals of Westwind Woods prepared for winter. A few remaining honey bees still gathered nectar on rarely warm afternoons. Ondrata, the muskrat, added more cattails and mud to his mound-like home. Odo and the other whitetails munched the meadow grass and kept putting on fall weight.

Ardea, the great blue heron, had deserted Westwind Woods as had Branta, his mate and their brood of Canada geese. The only local family of waterfowl that remained were Sponsa and his family, and they, too, would wing south soon.

Male wood ducks are North America's most colorful gamebird, and

Sponsa, a three-year old drake, was no exception. Early one morning, shortly after the town meeting, he preened his colorful feathers and splashed in the shallows of the Kenawabi River near the Grayson Road Bridge.

A hint of rising sun spread golden rays through the bare hardwoods and fell on the bright colors of the bathing wood duck. His gray-brown sides and blue-black back were separated by a band of white wing feathers. The purple sheen of his royal chest was dappled with triangle-shaped white spots. Like Phas, the ring-necked pheasant, Sponsa wore a white collar. His yellow bill with its crimson base and bright red eyes set off a handsome head of emerald and purple feathers and white face markings. The head feathers swept back to form a colorful tuft of these same colors.

Like certain other species, wood ducks have made a big comeback from low population levels of former years. Controlled hunting seasons and bag limits are a big reason. So are man's attempts to improve nesting habitat.

Wood ducks, or woodies as they are sometimes called, like to nest in the natural cavities of large trees. But these hollow trees are not always around and competition with owls, squirrels, raccoons and other wood ducks is often fierce. Wood ducks prefer flooded woods or thick timber along streams. They will quickly use man-made nests in the form of wooden boxes nailed to trees in such areas. Conservation clubs across the country have helped bring the wood duck back through such nest building projects. Sponsa, himself, was reared in such a man-made home not far from where he now played in the river shallows.

Breakfast was the next order of this new day, and Sponsa whistled to his mate nearby and their four young, as large as the parent birds, to join him in a flight to the marsh. The wood duck family burst from the river in a spray shower and cut through the hardwoods rather than follow the twisting course upstream.

In the lead, Sponsa dodged around bare maple, beech, oak and hickory. He felt the brisk autumn morning ruffling through his feathers, and he felt the urge to migrate more strongly this morning than ever before.

As the wood ducks streaked across the meadow, Sponsa caught a blur of movement in the marsh just ahead. In wood duck fashion, he zig-zagged left and then right and cut across the cattails at an angle away from the movement. Then he spotted the glint of sunlight on metal and was startled into panicked flight at several loud, crashing sounds.

"You got one, Dad," he heard a boy cry. Sponsa raced into the protective trees across the marsh and pond. His mate and the other three young followed close behind, their wings a blur of frantic motion. He led them to a little stream that trickled through thick woods to the river. The family dropped into a secluded pool to rest and recover from their fear.

Duck hunters in the marsh had now made it a hostile place to go. Sponsa and the other wood ducks would get a hasty breakfast of acorns from big oaks along this stream. Then they would take to the air and wing south without one of their family members.

Back in the marsh, Jerry Johnson, dressed in old chest waders two sizes too big for him, slogged through the cattails to retrieve his father's duck.

"It's a wood duck, Jerry," Mr. Johnson said, examining the bird at close range. "It's a young drake. As adults, they're beautiful birds."

Jerry's father wished his son had made the kill instead. This was Jerry's third duck hunting trip this season, and he had yet to score.

"Sorry I missed again, Dad," the husky youngster said. "Guess I need more practice on my lead."

Jerry and his father had been in the marsh since dawn, and the one wood duck was the only bird they had to show for their hunting efforts so far that day. A few floating mallard decoys bobbed in the pond.

"Let's get back in the blind," Mr. Johnson said. "Maybe we can talk down a passing mallard or two before the morning's gone."

Mr. Johnson was glad that he had a son now old enough to hunt. He and Jerry had taken a hunter's safety course together earlier that fall, and these hunting trips were important to build a good father-son relationship. Mr. Johnson knew that his son was not too interested in school, but the boy did enjoy hunting and fishing. These were two things they liked to do together. He poured a cup of steaming coffee from his red Thermos and sipped it slowly.

"Son, have you been studying that book on waterfowl identification I gave you?" he asked.

"I think I know most of the drakes now, Dad." Jerry said. "And I think I know the point totals, too."

"All right. How many points is that woody worth?"

"Well," Jerry began, "that's a 75-point duck, Dad. So you can't shoot another one, since you're only allowed 100 points total."

"That's right. What other ducks can't I shoot, son?"

"You can't shoot a black duck," Jerry said. "And, let's see, you can't shoot a hen mallard, either. The others I can't remember."

Jerry's father continued. "Redheads, canvasbacks and hooded mergansers are 75 or 100 point ducks, too, so I can't shoot them, either."

"That point system is weird," Jerry said. "Why can't we just shoot any old ducks we see?"

Jerry's father went on to explain that some species were not as plentiful as others with lower points. Other ducks like canvasbacks and redheads were becoming rare. He then told his son of the problems that nesting waterfowl face each spring.

"Predators, like crows and raccoons, get a lot of the eggs," he said. "And in Canada, in the prairie potholes of Manitoba, Saskatchewan and Alberta, where thousands of ducks nest, drought can ruin the duck crop. So can high water or late freeze-ups in the spring. Then, a lot of ducks don't make it down the flyways to their wintering grounds either. But I'll tell you something, son. If it wasn't for us duck hunters and groups like Ducks Unlimited, there wouldn't be any ducks around to shoot."

"Why's that?" Jerry wondered.

His father explained that in the 1920s and early 1930s, waterfowl populations in North America reached all-time lows. The reasons were greedy market hunting, poor nesting seasons and loss of habitat.

"Hunters have spent over $165 million in duck stamps since 1934 and spent $11 million last year alone," Mr. Johnson said. "The Fish and Wildlife Service buys wetlands with this money. That helps guarantee ducks for the future. Ducks Unlimited, like the group I belong to in Gratiot City, does the same thing."

"So hunters actually help the ducks, right, Dad?"

"That's right," Mr. Johnson said. "Hunting seasons and bag limits don't hurt the ducks, as a lot of people want you to believe. Take that family of wood ducks there. We took one out of six. Possibly one or two more will be taken by hunters this season. Next spring there will still be two and maybe more to nest again."

The sun rose higher, and the day began to warm. By midmorning, it looked as though no more ducks would pass over. Mr. Johnson began to think of the pile of leaves that needed raking in his yard. Jerry said something about getting a gang of friends together for a football game.

"Get down, son," Mr. Johnson suddenly said. "There's a little string of ducks coming up from the river toward us."

"What kind?" Jerry wondered.

"They look like mallards. Stay low and be quiet." Fumbling in his flannel shirt pocket, Mr. Johnson produced a hard, black rubber duck call. He quacked loudly with it and watched the flock of four mallards through the cattails around the burlap-wrapped blind.

"They're checking out the decoys, just out of range," Mr. Johnson announced. "The lead duck's a big greenhead mallard. If I can turn them around, you take him, son. Be sure to lead him, though."

He gave out with a series of calls, and the tight bunch of mallards swept over the meadow and then turned back toward the marsh. The sun glanced off the emerald head of a handsome drake in front. Mr. Johnson did not pick up his double-barrel shotgun.

"Be ready, son," he said to Jerry, who hunkered down in the blind. "Here they come, up the line, just as neat as pie." Jerry's father was whispering now, "Careful. Careful. Slip the safety off your gun. Get ready, O.K., start up. Now, son, now!"

Jerry leaped to his feet and, as his father told him, pulled up behind the flaring mallards, swept past the lead drake and in one smooth motion touched off a shot at the winging greenhead.

The big drake crumpled in midair and crashed to the pond with a loud splash. The other mallards raced for the river.

"I got him!" Jerry hollered. "I got my first duck, Dad!"

Jerry's father thumped him on the back. "A perfect shot, son!" he said proudly. "You did that just right. You made a clean kill, too."

Jerry leaped from the blind to retrieve his duck, which lay still on the rippling pond. Mr. Johnson watched his son for a long moment and thought about the first duck he had shot years ago. The blind was like this one, and Jerry's grandfather was along as witness.

CHAPTER 14

ODO

the White-Tailed Buck

early two months had passed since chain saws ripped the silence of Westwind Woods. Now, in early November, sunshine was a sometime thing, and gray dawns merged into gray days. Storm spitting rain and freezing nights were the order, and cold winds blew at the bare hardwoods. A harsh winter was in the making.

On one such nippy November morning 10 miles away in Gratiot City, a black-robed judge sat in his circuit court chambers. Judge Garver had been on the bench for many years and was highly respected by Bellecrest County citizens who returned him to office again and again. Rarely had the old judge been faced with easy decisions over his long career. The problem he faced now was very difficult.

He studied a suit from the woodcutters who believed they were being shut off from their living by the judge's earlier order which banned cutting in Westwind Woods. Included in their complaint was a copy of their contract with the County Board of Commissioners.

The old man removed his reading glasses and ran a smooth hand over his chin. That request certainly was a good argument, he thought to himself. Replacing the glasses, he studied the original suit by the Bellecrest County Conservation Club. This was the paper, signed by President Don Reynolds, that had caused the judge to force the cutters to stop, because stripping the woods could upset the ecology. That suit still had merit, too, the judge decided.

There also was a recent request from the DNR to grant more time for the EIS they were making for the county.

These were the three things on the judge's mind when a court clerk

popped into the old man's chambers with a cup of steaming black coffee.

Thanking him, the judge took a long sip and folded his ancient hands around the white porcelain cup. "You know, Bob," he said to the clerk, "this Westwind Woods issue is becoming a political hot potato. It's a good thing this isn't an election year because I think this fight is going to split the county before it's over."

"I believe you're right, Judge Garver," the clerk said. "The news services are picking up things almost every day and getting them in newspapers across the state. Did you know that the woodcutters are asking for union support from some of the factories here in Gratiot City?"

"Now, that I didn't know," Judge Garver said. "But I understand the conservation people are passing petitions around the county to stop the lake. I also hear the business groups are going to start petitions of their own, along with an advertising campaign, to get people behind the lake project."

"Looks like a bitter fight before it's over," the clerk said, walking out.

Alone again, Judge Garver took another long sip of black coffee. "That you can count on," he said, mostly to himself. He then signed an order granting the DNR an additional 30 days, until Dec. 10, to complete its study.

The judge had ordered the EIS because he thought the report would help him make the proper decision about Westwind Woods. The Bellecrest County Board of Commissioners should have an EIS anyway, he felt, since it had been granted money by the state. A task force of five experts from the DNR had been making the study, and the judge thought that 30 more days was enough time to complete the report.

One thing the task force would find out was the amount of pressure people using the proposed lake and park would put on the environment. On the other hand, it was hard to know how much people pressure existed now. Westwind Woods had been public land since Colonel West donated it to the county, and it was open for anybody to use. Hunters, fishermen, campers, hikers, snowmobilers and others used the land, but no one knew to what extent.

The animals knew, though, and if they could talk they would tell the task force that more and more people each year visited Westwind Woods. Philo, the woodcock; Branta, the Canada goose, and Phas, the ring-necked pheasant, were just some of the animals with stories to tell. Odo, the white-tailed buck, was another.

Once or twice each summer and fall, poachers tried to ambush the old buck as he entered the big meadow at dusk or by illegally jack lighting him with powerful flashlights at night as he fed in the open field. Odo had cunningly escaped each time.

The worst pressure of the year came during the last two weeks of November, though, during the statewide deer hunting season. Then, red-coated hunters sought Odo's handsome spread of dark antlers which this year boasted 10 curving points in a wide-spreading, almost perfect rack. Several people knew the wise old buck still lived in Westwind Woods. He had been seen often by other hunters and fishermen as he browsed in the big meadow. In a state where thousands of deer hunters travel to the northern woods for hunting each year, Odo had caused quite a stir in heavily populated Bellecrest County.

Nov. 15, the opening day of deer season, would dawn silent and cold. Hoarfrost tipped the remaining oak leaves in white. The clusters crackled in a slight pre-morning breeze as once glittering stars faded with the approaching dawn. There was not enough wind to stir the stiffened meadow grass, also white from the heavy frost, but deadened cattails clicked gently on the frozen pond.

Earlier that night, Odo and the other deer had fed heavily on meadow grass before the frost starched it white. The old buck had led his band of a half-dozen whitetails into the safety of the big hardwoods before first light.

As Odo led the deer out, a group of five hunters moved single file toward the meadow from the old West mansion where they had parked their cars. Their boots crunched the stiff carpet of grass, and their low voices carried in the still air. From the safety of the hardwoods, Odo looked over his shoulder. He saw their flashlights wink through naked trees as the hunters, in a single line, bobbed along the meadow trail.

Odo grew alarmed and took no chances whenever he saw, heard or smelled humans. He considered them all dangerous, whether they carried rifles or fishing rods. Pushing his band of whitetails, including one yearling spikehorn, ahead of him, Odo and the deer herd melted deeper into the woods.

Back in the meadow, growing light showed a silent, white world. The band of hunters had stopped, and together the five men formed a small huddle. Steam rose from each as they breathed and talked.

"See, what'd I tell you?" asked one heavy set man in a red snowmobile suit. He carried a rifle on a sling over his shoulder and pointed with his flashlight to the ground.

"That big buck was in here last night, just like I figured. There ain't no frost in his tracks here, so they're fresh."

"He probably slipped into the woods, Jack, just as we came along the trail," another red-suited hunter added.

Another man, kneeling, spread his fingers along Odo's wide track. "He must be something big," he said, looking up at the others.

"He is," Jack said bluntly. "And you better believe he's something smart, too!" Jack had hunted Odo the past two seasons and last year had missed the massive buck at close range.

"I was so nervous I drew circles instead of drawing down with my rifle," Jack had later joked. He hoped today for another chance and had organized the party of drivers for that purpose.

Unlike the poachers, Jack was a true sportsman who believed in the game laws. With his hunting skills, he and his friends might have bagged Odo out of season, as others had tried to do, but that thought was foreign to him. After all, how can one brag about a trophy deer killed out of season? Jack would do it right or not at all.

Jack's plan was to spread the five drivers into a horseshoe-shaped wedge and push north two miles toward the Grayson Road Bridge. He took the middle and placed the drivers, two to each side of him, about 200 yards apart. The man on his far left would walk the river bank downstream. The driver on his far right would skirt the old West mansion. The others were placed in between. Three more hunters waited near the cutover woods near Grayson Road Bridge. Jack's plan was to push the deer downriver, hoping for a shot along the way, and then pressure them into an ambush.

Each driver had a whistle, and Jack had told them to blow it every 20 steps or so. The noise would help to move the deer and would also let the other hunters know where everyone was. This was a safety idea as well as a good way to keep intact the horseshoe shape. Jack had told the men to push into the heavy thickets and to zig-zag along so as not to allow a smart buck like Odo to sneak back through the lines.

This was the day someone was going to collect that fine old buck, Jack had decided. Each of the men hoped, of course, that he would be the lucky hunter.

From the moment Odo heard the first shrill whistle blast, he knew that he and the others were being driven. He began to force the other deer ahead for a couple hundred yards but then stopped in a thick stand of poplar trees where blackberry vines grew in dense tangles. He wanted to know how many hunters were coming and exactly where they were.

A rising fear began to gnaw at him, but Odo fought down panic. These same events had occurred before, and he had always survived because of his intelligence. He suddenly became extra alert, dropping his head low into the tangles to hide his massive rack of horns and pricking his large ears straight up to catch the slightest sound.

The men made no effort to hide their noise, and Odo heard sticks break. He also heard the men's clothing swish through the dense tangles of saplings and vines. Blast after whistle blast cut the silence of the crisp November morning. Although the shrill noise made the buck's heart throb each time he heard them, the racket helped him to pinpoint the hunters' locations.

Crouching low in the forest tangle, Odo soon knew that he stood between two of the drivers. One hunter cut toward him for a few yards and then swung back the other way. Odo could see him 100 yards away, crashing through the woods. A rifle crooked in his arm, the man wore a blaze orange hunting vest, which to the color blind deer was just another shade of gray.

Odo crept from the thicket and stole away in the direction the other deer had taken. Keeping his huge horns low, the buck eased from one thicket to another for a half hour or so and tried to keep a couple hundred yards between him and the drivers. He made no noise, slipping along like a brown ghost, and watched for danger on all sides. The instinctive drive to live was a demand that his brain and nervous system made upon all of his senses. He remained tense and very alert while this dominating thought gripped him completely and shut out all other impulses.

Experience had made Odo smart. Through seven years of hunting seasons, the wise old buck had stayed alive by his wits. He had been chased as well as ambushed but had lived through it all. His survival was due to luck, too, especially as a young buck, but more recently his experience and smartness had helped him stay alive.

Odo stopped once to smell the tracks of the other deer, several of which were his wives and offspring. He saw where they had split up around a tangle of downed trees. Odo sniffed the scent of fear in their tracks and knew that the deer were running wildly in headlong flight as they panicked through the woods. A whistle blast came from nearby, and Odo quickly slipped into the fallen trees ahead.

He knew he was close to the Grayson Road Bridge, and he clearly remembered that the woods stopped where the woodcutters had cleaned it out upriver. Odo was very close to that point. It would be sure death to run across the open ground ahead, and the old buck knew he either had to find a hiding place here or sneak back through the drivers. Either way, the vise-like grip of hunters moved closer to him. Odo felt the pressure of their trap.

Before him the log jam was thick. Odo squirmed his way into its very center and lay hidden under a toppled pine tree. It would be hard to find him in here. The whistle sounds and breaking of sticks rang loudly in his brain. His breath began to come in painful, short gasps, and he heard voices hollering back and forth. A moment later, Odo jerked hard when he heard a loud rifle blast from the direction of the Kenawabi River.

He lay perfectly still in the dense tangle even when the voices and other noises centered along the river. After a time, he again heard something coming closer. He could tell from the footsteps and scraping of clothing that the noise was from a hunter, and then a second man and a third. He heard voices, too, more clearly than ever. Odo wormed his way even deeper under the pine log and listened carefully.

"That spikehorn and two does tried to cross the river right in front of lucky Max," one of the men said. The three hunters leaned their guns against an oak and sat on stumps and trees of the logjam. Thirty feet away in its center, Odo lay still, his eyes unblinking. The deer's heart pounded violently, and he was having trouble getting a measured breath.

"Yeah, I saw Max's deer," Jack said. "That's a nice buck and he made a clean kill. Nobody saw anything of the old boy, though, huh?"

"If we had snow, we could track him," the third hunter said.

"Sometimes I think that deer walks on air," Jack said. "I'll bet you my gun that one of us walked within a couple of rods of that big buck, and he just lay hidden, cool as a cucumber, and watched us go by."

Odo, of course, could not understand what the men were saying. Their voices, so close to where he lay hidden in the log tangle, nearly drove him into a panic. He kept fighting the fear within him and lay still, for how much longer he did not know.

"The heck of it is," the first hunter said, "somebody will come along and shoot him out of season."

"Maybe not," Jack replied. "The season is two weeks long, and we'll be back. Let's go round up the other boys and hunt somewhere else this afternoon."

Jack slung his rifle over his back again and led the others toward the river and the rest of the hunters. He smiled to himself as he thought about how the deer had slipped away again. His desire to bag the old buck was nothing personal. It was the challenge of hunting him that interested Jack. The sport was in trying to outwit the deer, not in shooting him.

Jack knew that he was not a greedy hunter. Once he had hidden in some cattail marshes and watched a flock of Canada geese, as big as boxcars, as they swarmed right over his head. They were so royal, so wild, that for a moment he could not shoot one. He never regretted not pulling the trigger that day many years ago. Yet the hunting scene still burned in his mind as sharply as though it happened yesterday.

He was a true sportsman because he obeyed the hunting laws, but most importantly he respected the game he hunted. The thought had occurred often to him that if he and the old buck should ever cross paths again, he might not be able to kill the deer. Sometimes he wondered if last year's miss was on purpose.

The others looked upon Jack as an expert hunter. Jack knew that he had a reputation to uphold, and because the others probably could not understand how he sometimes felt he would not venture to tell them. A sportsman does not hunt game just for the thrill of killing it, and Jack was a sportsman. He might or might not kill the old buck if he ever had the chance again. It was his decision alone and he would make it alone. Jack chuckled again to himself as he thought about it.

"What's so funny, Jack?" one of the others asked.

"Oh, I was just thinking about how excited Max must have been when that spikehorn buck busted from the woods right on top of him," Jack said.

CHAPTER 15

PROCYON
the Raccoon

hanksgiving at Ellen Nisbet's house was a big affair this year. Steve's grandparents came from out of state. His favorite aunt—Ellen's sister—and her two boys and girl about the ages of Ellen's children also arrived for a weekend visit.

It was a family reunion, made more happy because of the turkey dinner and long holiday weekend. Like Steve and the other kids, Ray had no classes, and he spent the time with his parents and sisters. A couple of times the family talked about the planned Westwind Lake, and Ray's bitterness about the idea quickly surfaced.

"You're dead set against this lake, aren't you, son?" his father, an important looking gentleman in his mid-50s, remarked one evening.

"Dad, it's wrong to tear down woods like that," Ray said, "no matter what the reason. We've got to take stands against the ruining of natural habitat in this country, and we've got to do it now."

"Well, I've always believed in conservation," the elder Moore said, "and I've tried to teach you kids right from wrong."

"You did," Ray said. "And you also taught us to stand up for what we believe is right. But we'll wait for the results of the EIS and then see what the county does with it."

"When is that due?" Mr. Moore asked.

"Two weeks from tomorrow, Dad," Ray said.

Cold rain fell off and on over the long weekend, and most of the time the family stayed indoors and visited. Outside, in the natural world, the animals adjusted to the changing season and the coming of winter.

Odo had made it through another hunting season after a couple more

close calls. He and his band of whitetails hid in the thickets of Westwind Woods by day and only dared creep into open areas when darkness brought safety. Corvus and other crows from miles around began to group together in their pine roost downriver toward Grayson Road Bridge. For the next few months, they would gather here each night in the comfort of the big pines and sleep away cold winter nights.

Many of the animals of Westwind Woods were nocturnal; that is, they hunted for food at night. Owls, opossums, foxes, skunks and raccoons are just a few of the nocturnal animals that lived there. Food was harder to find now that winter was at hand, and many of the animals had to look harder than before for something to eat.

One such animal was Procyon, the raccoon. Now about three-quarters grown and weighing nearly 10 pounds, Procyon spent his nights wandering up and down the Kenawabi River. He was always trying to satisfy both his curiosity and his hunger. He had been raised with a litter of five raccoons born last spring and, like his brothers and sisters, was now on his own.

Raccoons are one of nature's most interesting creatures. Their curious habits make them check into nearly everything in their nightly travels. Procyon had a habit of poking his mask-like face and human-shaped paws into river bank holes and under overhanging banks. He liked to thrust his nose into debris piles of leaves and logs along the river, and he completely explored every little stream and spring that trickled into the Kenawabi River.

Procyon would eat almost anything. Field corn and farmers' vegetables were a favorite food as were all types of wild berries. He had learned to pin frogs with his quick hands in the marsh and how to catch the backward swimming crayfish as they moved over gravel bars in the river.

Clams were a delicacy to Procyon, too, and early in their training the parent raccoons had taught their young how to crack open the clam shells and scoop out the white meat inside. Next summer, he would eat insects and mice and would never turn down wild honey or birds' eggs if he chanced upon them.

Raccoons are very smart animals and can be vicious fighters, especially when threatened by dogs or men. Even so, many have been tamed and even taught to do tricks. They should never be taken from the wild, though, as this is usually against the law.

Raccoons have long been prized for their fur and meat. Hunters and trappers seek their heavy, gray-brown hides and ring-striped tails. The pelts are made into raccoon coats, gloves and Davy Crockett caps. Others are just as interested in the meat as in pelts. The meat can taste like pork or beef, depending upon how it is cooked.

If Procyon was a full-grown raccoon, he might easily have been shot earlier that fall. A pack of coon hounds had treed him in a tall poplar near the pond one October night. They had picked up his hot track along the river bank mud, and when Procyon heard their excited bawls and squeals, he hurried toward the marsh.

The long-legged 'coon dogs, a pair of bawling blueticks and a ranging black and tan hound with a full-throated chop to his voice, closed in fast on

Procyon. The young raccoon barely made it to the safety of the poplar where he sprinted for some upper branches. Below, the leaping hounds snarled and snapped at the masked runaway.

Arriving soon, the hunters knew from their dogs' howls that they had treed a raccoon. They beamed their powerful flashlights in Procyon's face, and the glare was painful to his eyes.

"Small 'coon," one of the men said. "Let him be. Maybe we'll take him next year when he's full-grown."

That event was the only time Procyon had seen dogs or people. That is, until one rainy night during the Thanksgiving weekend.

Procyon had been scouting upriver since nightfall, and his tracks littered the east side of the Kenawabi River. The small, hand-like prints were everywhere on soft sand bars. Feeling with his paws through the gravel bottom of a shallow section of stream, Procyon seized a clam. Using his sharp nails and strong jaws, he cracked open the treasure. He scooped out the meat, and in raccoon fashion washed his food in the river. This was not to clean the food, as many people believe, but was to wet the treat so that he might eat it more easily.

During those darkest hours of night, sometime between midnight and dawn, Procyon wandered away from the river toward Riverside Subdivision. The steady pattering of raindrops had finally stopped, and a light mist was in the blowing night air. The young raccoon mounted the hill that slanted from the cluster of homes to the river below. Once on top, he saw the street lights of the human world before him.

Procyon shook the water from his coat, and with his nose to the ground ambled toward the houses. The lights interested him, and he wanted to see what lay in this exciting world of night lights.

At the end of the street where the turn-around began, someone had parked a shining red car. Procyon scooted to the bright object, shining from the soft glare of a street light. He sniffed the gasoline odor from under the trunk and smelled the tires. He was dazzled with the bright wet chrome, which danced like bright diamonds under the swaying street light, and he was surprised at how smooth it was to his touch.

From here, Procyon wandered through the neighborhood and, like some detective, checked everything that he came across. A child's plastic wheeled toy got a careful going over as did a day old newspaper on the front porch of a ranch home.

When Procyon ducked around the back of Ellen's home, the bright mercury light mounted on her television antenna picked him up. He tried to scale the wooden posts of the patio deck, and the scraping noises his claws made awakened Ray's sleeping Labrador retriever.

Spotting the raccoon, Jet, the black dog, growled deeply and charged from his house. He got as far as the chain snapped to his collar would allow before being jerked to a sudden stop. In anger, he snarled and then began barking loudly as Procyon scampered to a nearby beech tree and rushed up the smooth bark.

The raccoon knew he was safe in this tree, but his heart pounded wildly and his breath came in painful gasps. He well remembered being treed a few weeks ago and was frightened at Jet's loud growls and fierce barking.

The back porch light came on suddenly, and Ray, slipperless and dressed in jeans pulled over his pajama bottoms, appeared on the patio deck.

"Jet, shut up!" he ordered. "What's the matter with you, anyway? You'll wake up the whole neighborhood!"

Jet flattened back his ears and slunk his head low while Ray bawled him out. He did not like to hear his master speak angrily to him. He dropped his tail between his hind legs and sulked with downcast eyes.

"Get in the house, Jet!" Ray blurted. "Go on, get in your house and shut up that racket."

Jet took one long look at the beech where Procyon was hiding somewhere on the dark side and shook with excitement. Then he obeyed his master and slowly disappeared into the white dog house. Here he flopped his head down in the straw and whimpered his disappointment. Ray went into the house and the porch light snapped off.

Still frightened, Procyon hid in the dark shadows for several minutes before sneaking down the back side of the tree. He hit the ground running and dashed off into the neighborhood.

Soon he was back to his detective work, and very little missed his attention. A couple blocks down the street and an hour later, he found an open side door to someone's garage. Snooping inside, he found a garbage can half-filled and smelling of food. When Procyon reached up, he tipped the metal container over with a loud crash and sent its insides scattering over the cement floor. He was searching through some egg shells when the lights came on all around him. A wild-eyed woman dressed in a red housecoat stormed into the garage.

"Get out of here, you varmint!" she screamed half out of fear and half out of anger. She struck at the raccoon with a broom and shooed him out the side door.

Procyon was more frightened than the woman, and he bolted for the safety of the night. Once outside, he ran straight for the river and did not look back. He had learned that the world of humans was not safe, and he must not go back.

Although Procyon could not understand the meaning or the reason, animals always suffer when their boundaries overlap with the human world.

CHAPTER 16

ONDATRA
the Muskrat

 mixed weather bag marked the passing of November into December. These late fall-early winter days are often an uncertain time of year. Rain can change from sleet to hail to snow and back again to partly sunny skies all in the course of an early December day.

As the soil freezes and thaws, frost action heaves rocks to the ground in old pastures, fields and lawns. Ice on the ponds and lakes is sometimes glassy smooth and sometimes topped with slush. Gravel roads are frozen iron-like one day and rutted with mudholes the next.

In a few more weeks, winter would lay complete claim to Westwind Woods and blanket the land in total whiteness. But for now winter's bid was not strong enough, and the woods and fields were scars of white and brown, gray and black. The weather seemed unable to make up its mind whether to hold autumn in check or to release it to winter.

At this time of year, a careful eye was needed to find beauty in such drab surroundings. Each of the months and seasons has a beauty of its own, though. Even on the dullest December days when storm clouds spat sleet from lead-colored skies, the distant woods were an eye-catching smoky gray. They were handsome on the river's east side where bare beech, hickory and oak topped each other in gentle swells. On the west side, most of the farmers' fields lay brown and untilled, waiting for the spring plow to start life again. And in a couple of fields, bright green winter wheat popped above the brown earth and gave a pleasing color contrast. Through this changing scene, the Kenawabi River slowly threaded its black, icy water.

Another kind of beauty—the close-up kind—also exists in fall/winter

woods, but many people are in too much of a hurry to see it. A walk through Westwind Woods, for example, at this time of year would reveal much to the person who looked carefully about him.

Sciurus, the squirrel, could still be seen hiding acorns under oak leaves. Along fence rows that straddled the barren fields maroon clusters of dogwood thickets grew. Here Phas and the other pheasants and Colinus, the quail, scratched among the leaves for fallen, white dogwood berries.

From the outside the marsh and pond looked lifeless, too. Freezing nights and sleeting days had pulled the living greenness from the marsh grass and cattail stalks which were now brown and brittle. The cattail heads were mostly split open and their cotton-like insides were scattered throughout the marsh. All the ducks had flown south by now and even Ardea, the great blue heron, always among the last to leave, had departed the marsh weeks ago.

Under the ice, which grew in thickness as winter approached, a slowed-down state of life still went on. The chunky bass and bluegills, although not as active as in warmer months, still swam slowly in search of food. Painted turtles, frogs and crayfish buried themselves in the bottom mud and slept away the numbing cold.

One animal that was active all winter long was the muskrat. These robust little creatures with their warm, chestnut colored fur coats and black, rat-like tails played and looked for food each day, no matter how bad the weather became.

The pond and marsh were home to several dozen muskrats whose cone-shaped huts dotted the brown marsh like sod houses on the prairie. Beginning in early fall, muskrats collect cattails, mud, sticks and marsh grass to build winter homes. Some of the bigger huts stand four or five feet above the marsh and house several muskrats at once.

On cold nights, the muskrats huddle together in these marsh vegetation houses, and their body heat helps to warm the inside. The homes are carefully built just above the waterline. They have two or three underwater entrances that never freeze. Dead vegetation helps insulate the house from bitter cold, and the animals' body heat also helps to keep the waterways open all winter.

Ondatra lived in such a house right at the marsh edge where it met the deeper pond. It was a sturdy house that he, his mate and members of their last litter had built that fall. The younger muskrats, born in September, were nearly full-grown now and next spring would leave their parents and begin families of their own.

Sometimes ice welded the pond and marsh tight shut for several weeks at a time. The muskrats would then be trapped in their own homes, but that was no cause for worry. Unless the animals overpopulated, enough food in the form of cattail roots, underwater plantlife and mussels existed for them to eat.

Muskrats use certain runways under the ice. These can usually be found by looking for streams of air bubbles or by trying to find tunnel-like canals in the soft bottom mud. Muskrats are strong swimmers. They use their large, webbed hind feet as paddles and their tapered tails, sometimes nearly as long as their roly-poly bodies, to steer by.

These animals can stay underwater for three to five minutes. They know the exact location of each air hole in the ice or pocket of air trapped under the ice. Being locked under several inches of ice and snow does not bother muskrats at all.

Muskrats are safer under the ice than they are in warmer months. In the summer, foxes, hawks and owls prey on them, but they cannot get to the muskrats as easily in winter. Wild mink, which sometimes attack muskrats right in their marsh homes and bankside dens along the river, are the only natural enemy that muskrats have to fear year around.

Muskrat pelts are valuable, and hundreds of thousands of the animals are trapped across the U.S. each fall and winter. Their dark, long-haired pelts are used in coats, hats and gloves.

Man was the real danger that Ondatra and the others faced now, other than the mink. In late November each year, the trapping season opened.

Recently a trapper had visited the marsh every day and had already caught many muskrats. An older man who lived in Bellecrest village, he had trapped Westwind Woods and streams and ponds in other parts of the county for many years. The trapper was very efficient at this sport that he loved so much.

A retired factory worker, the man owned a green canoe that he put into the river at the old iron bridge in Bellecrest each day. As he floated downstream toward Grayson Road, he would check and reset his traps on both banks for mink, muskrat and raccoon. Beaching his canoe at the small stream that drained the pond, the man would leave the river to check his sets in the pond and marsh.

Each day, he wore rubber hip boots, thick corduroy pants pulled over insulated underwear and a red and black checked woolen shirt. On nasty days, he pulled an olive-colored parka over his shirt. On his back, he always carried a packbasket full of traps, wire, apples, lures, a hatchet and other trapping gear.

It had been a good year, and the man was very satisfied with his catch of fur. Two back to back mild winters had been easy on furbearing animals in this region. The large number of animals left for seed in the spring had helped produce bumper crops the following fall. This year might very well be a record harvest for the trapper.

He thought about this one day as he beached his canoe in the wet sand, relighted his worn pipe and shouldered his heavy pack once more. A rough winter was in the making this year. The man knew that weeks of ice, snow and freezing temperatures would shut off many of the animals from their food supplies. Winter was early this year, and it would probably be late in leaving next spring.

That meant that many animals would die this year from lack of food. This prediction made his business of being a trapper more important than ever. Many people view the trapper as cruel. They think trapping, as well as hunting, should be illegal. Little do they know that an always changing and delicate habitat can support only a certain number of animals each year. The surplus, if not harvested, would be lost to disease and starvation.

The man knew that it was better to trap the animals and make use of their meat and hides than to let them be wasted. Although many thought of the steel trap as a tool of torture, the man also knew better. When water trapping for mink, muskrat and raccoon, he was very careful to make only drowning sets so that the animals he caught would suffer very little. He doubted that a trapped animal felt much more than numbness anyway since many times he had come upon them asleep in his traps. Still, he took no chances and made only drowning sets.

The man's methods were far less cruel than slow, painful death by starvation or disease, which often result when there are too many animals. Conservation laws protect the animals from unfair means of collecting them. For example, seasons, limits and other restrictions help control the sports of hunting, fishing and trapping. They are the laws the sportsman agrees to accept when he buys a license.

A trapper has other, unwritten laws that he must follow, too, and the visitor to Westwind Woods was careful to abide by these, too. For example, he checked his traps each day just in case a live animal might be in one. Another practice he followed was to give the animal a sporting chance. He did this by keeping his sets away from their cone-shaped homes in the marsh and burrows along the riverbank. Finally, the man was careful not to overtrap an area and always left enough animals for seed.

Many people don't believe in trapping and in some states are attempting to stamp it out. The way the man figured it, he had a right to trap, but along with that right came the duty to do it wisely, carefully and legally. This the man had done for many years as he ran his trapline up and down the Kenawabi River.

Reaching the marsh one day in early December, the man tested the strength of the ice with a walking staff he usually carried. Satisfied that it would support his weight once more, he moved from set to set. The man had changed from open water methods to under the ice trapping which was much more difficult. Most of his sets consisted of traps set in runways under the ice. In deeper water in the pond, he made platform bait sets for muskrats.

A couple of these held drowned muskrats today. The man thought to himself that he had never seen so many 'rats in the marsh before. In two weeks' time, he had already caught an amount equal to a normal season's catch.

The platform sets were simple to make. The man used a log about as long and thick as a small fence post. He nailed a couple of spikes into the log to make a platform for his trap, which he then secured to the log with the use of a fence staple through the trap ring. Above the trap he wired a piece of apple or carrot for bait. Then, cutting a hole in the ice, he shoved the log into the bottom mud at a 45-degree angle.

Muskrats swimming by would see the bait and walk up the log to get at it. They would become caught and drown right away.

The man made such a set a few yards out into the pond from Ondatra's house. The trapper knew that several muskrats lived in the hut. In fact, he had caught one of Ondatra's offspring several days before in a nearby feedbed set. He hoped to catch one of the larger, parent muskrats with his freshly made platform set.

The man heaped up what snow he could gather and packed it over the hole. This might help keep the hole from freezing tonight and make tomorrow's job of checking the trap a little easier.

It was already midafternoon. Since the man had a couple miles of river to float before his take-out point at the Grayson Road Bridge, he wasted no time. Shouldering his pack again, he walked briskly toward the river.

Inside their earthen mound, Ondatra, his mate and five of their offspring had listened to the dull sounds and occasional cracking of ice as the man walked about the pond. Ondatra did not know enough to fear the noises. He only knew that something large was walking on the ice, but he also knew that he was safe in his home. That was why he and his family slept away the afternoon and only shifted in their sleep when they heard the ice crack from the trapper's weight.

A few hours later darkness clamped shut on Westwind Woods. Feeling hunger and sensing that the night had come, Ondatra led his mate and youngsters in single file out the main runway. He swam with eyes open, eyes that already were well adjusted to darkness. Ondatra stopped at a spot along the marsh edge. Spotting a lone cluster of cattails, he dug fiercely with strong front paws and uprooted a stalk. He was lucky to find something so quickly to eat as food in the marsh was rapidly being eaten by the many muskrats. With the fat, potato-like tuber in his mouth, Ondatra swam fast back to the house. Several of the smaller muskrats followed him.

While the muskrat family chewed on sweet cattail roots, Ondatra's mate searched the pond bottom for some plantflife to eat. A couple of times she shot to the ice-capped surface where she drew quick breaths from an air hole. So far, she had found nothing to eat.

On one dive, the female swam past the platform set made by the trapper only hours before. She stopped at its base and then, looking up, spied a white slice of apple. Ondatra's mate walked up the slanted log. Just as she reached for her treat, the trap snapped shut with a metal click and rush of water.

Frantic, the female muskrat reared back and dove for the pond bottom. She got a couple of feet before the chain tightened and jerked her to a halt, suspending her like a clock pendulum. It was not pain, but fear, that sharpened her senses to a razor edge. The powerful trap jaws had clamped down tightly on her front paw, and she could not pull free.

In a desperate effort, the female bit and clawed at the steel that bound her. But the trapper had made his set carefully. With little suffering, this muskrat would drown quickly, and tomorrow the man would add her to others in his packbasket.

Trappers from generations before this man—back two centuries to the mountain men and to the Indians a thousand years before them—had harvested the furbearing animals of North America. His sport was a rich tradition, steeped in history and lore, one that he continued by setting his traps each year.

And what still might seem like a cruel game to some actually was a blessing in disguise. This was most true this year when food shortages in the wild were already being felt. The almanacs and weather forecasters alike were predicting a bitter winter of deep snows and record low temperatures.

CHAPTER 17

Meph
the Skunk

L ike the closing pages of a good book, December was over too soon. The short winter days and long, cold nights passed, and with the end of the month came the close of another year.

The always too-short Christmas vacation was a big reason. For Steve, the two-week school break was just a blur of events. Aunts, uncles and cousins had come and gone over the holidays. The reds and greens of Christmas and the cooking smells of baked ham and mince pies were over until next year. Much snow had made for a good vacation, and Steve and his friends had spent nearly every day outdoors tobogganing and skiing.

On the first morning back to school in early January, Jerry complained the loudest. It was bitter cold, the kind of cold that numbs fingers quickly and causes chimney smoke to belch straight up. When the yellow school bus with ice-rimed windows crunched to a halt in front of the milling students, Jerry was the last to board. "I hate yellow," he muttered and then to the driver, "How long until Easter vacation?"

Steve was glad to be getting back to school. Mrs. Rachel, the science teacher, had promised to teach her class how to stuff animals if someone brought in a good specimen. Frozen hard in a brown paper sack was a barn pigeon—a perfect bird for taxidermy, Steve thought.

He had shot the gray bird with green breast feathers and black wing bars a couple of days before in Farmer Greene's barn. High in the rafters of the musty barn, gloomy light made shapes uncertain. Even so, the pigeon had lined up perfectly in the peepsight of Steve's new pellet gun. Only one shot was needed to tumble the pigeon from his rafter perch to the hay strewn, concrete floor.

The gun was a Christmas present from Uncle Ray, who was with his nephew when Steve shot the plump pigeon.

"Next summer, we'll enroll you in a hunter's safety course," Ray had said. "And next Christmas, if you continue to show respect for guns and game, I'll talk to your mother about a new shotgun."

His very own shotgun. Seated in the bouncing school bus, Steve stroked the cold feathers of his frozen pigeon. He thought again, as he had a hundred times already, about what Uncle Ray had said. The white farmland rolled by as the bus bounced along.

Both the weather forecasters and almanacs were correct so far in predicting a severe winter. Westwind Woods had been snow-covered since mid-December, and each new snowfall added another white blanket upon earlier layers. Frigid arctic air blew at the bare trees, and the mercury stayed well below freezing day after day. The normal mid-January thaw would not come this year. Several more weeks would pass before bare earth and melting temperatures came again.

The cold season is a yearly hardship for northern animals everywhere. That's why they grow warm coats and build up fat reserves in the fall to help carry them through this season of hunger and hardship.

The owls and foxes could not get at the muskrats. Even the abundant field mice were harder to catch than ever. The big predators were forced to turn to quail, rabbits and pheasants for food. By midwinter, these animals were not as plentiful as they had been in the fall.

On more than one bone-chilling January morning, Bubo, the great horned owl, flew on an empty stomach to his lofty perch high in a twisted hickory tree. If snow stayed on the ground into February, his hunting chores would be doubly hard. Either he or his mate would have to take turns sitting on their eggs high in the hickory tree nest. Great horned owls are the first of the birds to mate. Often in early March, when their two or three young are born, sleet storms rake the trees, and the nights remain freezing.

Some animals, of course, migrate to warmer lands and others are true hibernators. Snakes, frogs, turtles and some mammals sleep away the cold. Their heartbeats and breathing slow down and body temperatures drop. Others like Procyon, the raccoon; Taxus, the badger, and Marmoth, the woodchuck, do not really hibernate, but they will stay in their dens during a cold snap for several days at a time.

Winter is the time when only the strong survive. The weak and diseased animals are the first to die off. Although this truth might seem cruel, it is nature's way of keeping only the healthy and strong for breeding stock in the spring. This also keeps animals from overpopulating beyond the land's ability to support them.

Some animals, especially omnivorous ones, don't fare so poorly in deep snow or cold temperatures. An omnivorous animal is one that will eat almost anything. Animals like skunks and opossums and birds like Corvus, the crow, often have an easier time than most since they will eat plantlife or animals, both dead and alive.

Meph, the skunk, for example, had suffered little hardship so far this winter. Although there were no insects for him to eat, as in the summer, there were plenty of mice to catch around his den in the rock foundation of

Farmer Greene's barn. The corncrib offered plenty of field corn. And he would never turn up his nose at table scraps left frozen in the dog's dish. In the fields were other mice, weed seeds and scattered grain that the automatic pickers had missed. Supper was nearly anything that Meph could find to eat. That meant chicken eggs and even young chicks if he could get at them.

Late one cold January afternoon, iron gray storm clouds, pushed by a face-numbing wind, swept across Westwind Woods. The snow that began to fall was hard packed. To the children getting off the school bus, it stung like birdshot as the wind flung it at them. By dusk, the wind was driving the snow—blizzard snow as it is sometimes called—almost horizontally. It was difficult to see very far. Such blizzards were not common in the southern part of the state, but then this was not a common winter, either.

As the light began to fail for another day and as he felt gnawings of hunger in his stomach, Meph stirred inside his den. He awoke, stretched several times inside his small, warm cavity in the rock wall and then poked his head outside.

Snow swirled around the edges of Farmer Greene's old red barn. Out across the field it was a blur of moving white. Meph would look for food close to home tonight. When he stepped out into the snowstorm, wind gusts puffed at his black and white striped body, lifting the thick fur. He entered the barn through a hole where a plank was missing and right away shuffled to a hay mound on the concrete. Here, he might quickly turn up a couple mice and finish supper early tonight.

Meph was almost two years old. He had been born in a den near one of the old pastures by the river. Being a male skunk, Meph lived alone in the winters and would seek a mate, very likely the same one he had last year, in a few more weeks when warmer temperatures brought the first faint signals of spring.

Skunks have few enemies. When they are babies, a very hungry owl or fox might attempt to scoop one up. Although skunk pelts are valuable, few trappers go after them. Only a farmer, angry at losing eggs or chicks, or a senseless hunter might try to shoot a skunk.

The reason is simple. Skunks have powerful scent glands and twin ports near the base of their tails. When a skunk turns his back and lifts his striped tail, watch out. He can emit a fine, mistlike spray for several feet. This burns the eyes and can cause sudden blindness. The odor may last for several weeks, too. No wonder most thinking creatures will not tangle with a skunk.

Meph only found one mouse in the haystack even though he waited patiently until full darkness. As he ate the mouse inside the cold barn, he could hear the wind howl outside. Some pigeons huddled together and cooed from the rafters above. In a cattle section through the wall behind him, Meph heard the impatient stamping of the Holstein cattle as they waited for supper.

When Farmer Greene entered the barn to feed them, Meph slipped quietly outside. It was inky dark by now, the only light coming from a mercury lamp over the front of the barn. Looking up, Meph watched a sea of moving snow being driven across the lighted barnyard. He headed for the field in an attempt to find supper quickly and get back to his warm den.

Another animal, also looking for food, was in the snow-packed field. Vulpes, the cross fox, had been sleeping all afternoon in a tight ball along a slope near the river. He had kept his long, thick tail over his nose to protect it from the biting cold. The storm had wakened him, and, like Meph, instinct told him to find supper fast and return to shelter until the storm blew over.

Neither animal was aware of the other until they almost collided in the night. Meph quickly turned his back to Vulpes and raised his big striped tail. Vulpes sprang back for a better look at this strange black and white creature. Keeping a few feet away and with head low, he began to circle the skunk for a better look. They looked like dancing partners as the fox tip-toed around Meph. Holding on to his scent, the skunk moved with him and kept his rear end hiked high. When Vulpes changed directions and moved the other way, Meph stayed right even with him.

Vulpes remembered seeing skunks before, but his parents had always ignored them. Of course, that was in the summer when food was plentiful. The hunger pangs reminded Vulpes that he had yet to eat tonight. So the young fox moved in closer to see if this animal was fair game.

Meph raised his striped flag even higher. All animals learn by experience, and tonight poor Vulpes would learn the hard way not to fool with skunks. Vulpes rushed in quickly to knock the skunk over. That's when Meph jetted his scent.

The powerful musk hit Vulpes squarely in the face, searing his eyes. The fox howled in pain and ran blindly across the snow-driven field. He could not see and stumbled in a blind panic. He had never felt pain like this, nor had he ever been so frightened. Even after several minutes of running and yelping, his eyes still burned. He finally stopped and rubbed his face in the snow. This action eased the pain a little, and he began to roll in the snow to rid his coat of the strong odor. Little did he know that the scent would last for several weeks. Even a couple of months later, if he happened to get his coat wet, the smell would still be there.

After a few minutes more, his vision began to clear, and the pain let up some more. Frustrated and dropping his tail between his legs like a fallen flag, the young fox whimpered. He faded into the snow-blinded night and tried to find a hillside protected from the howling wind. Here, he would curl up in a ball, hungry and sad, until another night of hunting came.

Meph, too, had had enough excitement for one night, and the skunk ambled back to the barnyard. With luck, perhaps he could knock over Farmer Greene's garbage can and rummage through it for something to eat. Meanwhile, the storm grew in fury and snow began to pile up in the woods and fields and in the streets of Bellecrest.

"Looks like there won't be school tomorrow, kids," Ellen Nisbet called from the kitchen.

Sitting in the dining room, Steve watched the snow slant across the patio deck outside. Ray oiled an old fishing reel whose parts lay scattered on the dining table.

"Now, tell me once more, Uncle Ray," Steve said. "What does EIS stand for?"

"Environmental Impact Study," Ray answered. "It's something the state government does to find out what might happen to the plant life and animal life of an area if an area is changed in any way."

"And the judge said that a lot of animals in Westwind Woods would die if they keep cutting the trees. Right, Uncle Ray?"

"Well," Ray started, "the results of the EIS proved that. So Judge Garver made his order permanent and stopped all cutting."

"But in science class Mrs. Rachel said this whole thing's not over yet," Steve offered. "They still might end up building a lake there anyway."

Ray sighed. "Yes, I know, Steve," he said.

Just then the doorbell rang. "Now, who in the world would be dropping by on such a night?" Ellen wondered aloud.

Steve sprang to the door, and amid a swirl of snow and rush of cold air Mr. Reynolds stepped in. His brown hat was speckled with snow, and he smacked his gloved hands together. "That wind's howling like something alive," he said.

"I can't stay but a minute," Mr. Reynolds added, turning down Ellen's offer of hot coffee. "The phones are out around here, and I've got some great news I knew Ray would want to hear."

"I seem to have lost a screw to my reel here," Ray said, holding up the reel. "I could stand to hear good news. Sit down and tell me."

"Well, the County Board of Commissioners cut short their meeting tonight because of the storm," Mr. Reynolds began. "Several of us from the conservation club were there, and we gave them our petitions supporting the judge's ban."

Ray cut in. "Wasn't it last week, Don, that the business group presented **their** petitions to the board to go ahead with the lake anyway?"

"That's right and that's why I've got great news," Mr. Reynolds said. "The board feels there are enough folks in this county on both sides to take the issue directly to them in a special March election. They decided tonight to seek an election."

Ray set the reel on the table. "You know, Don, that's the **only** fair way to ever decide what to do with Westwind Woods," he said. "Let the people decide."

"Exactly, but that's not all," the visitor went on. "The board also plans to ask the voters for one mill of tax to support recreation in the county. Do you see what that means, Ray?"

"I sure do," Ray said, a big smile spreading across his face. "The voters could say no to the lake project and yes to the millage plan. Then the county would have enough money and the people's support to turn Westwind Woods into a nature preserve and protect it."

"Right on. And that's why I'm calling a special meeting of the Bellecrest County Conservation Club for Thursday night. In less than two months we've got to inform a lot of people if we're going to win at the polls."

"I'll be at the meeting," Ray said. "And, Don, you're right. This is great news!"

CHAPTER 18

SITTA
the Nuthatch

llen Nisbet's prediction about school being closed was correct. The savage storm did not blow itself out until late afternoon of the next day. In its fury, it left cars stranded in ditches and schools and businesses closed. Sixteen inches of drifting new snow clogged roads shut around Bellecrest County. It would be a few days before snowplows cleared them and everything returned to normal.

Like most people, wild animals wait in their homes until a storm blows itself out. Rabbits and mice dig tunnels in the drifts and bury themselves, their body heat keeping them warm. Procyon, the raccoon; Meph, the skunk; Taxus, the badger, and Marmoth, the woodchuck, all had slumbered in their dens while the storm raged outside. In a tangle of sumac along a gentle river slope, Vulpes, the cross fox, had wrapped himself into a tight ball of red-brown fur. He slept poorly, awakening now and then to shake off the snow.

Some animals, especially birds, like to gather together during such storm conditions. Colinus and a dozen other bob-whites slept in a ring-shaped covey with all heads facing outside to watch for danger. Phas and several other ring-necked pheasants, hens and roosters alike, found cover in a dense thicket at the end of a field.

Finding food during the storm was hard and would still be a tough chore now that the blizzard had stopped. Steve was glad when it was over that he still had a little daylight left. That would give him time to clean out the snow from his bird feeder and restock it with food.

This was the second year that Steve had fed the winter birds. He and his family liked to watch the different types—blue jays, nuthatches, tufted

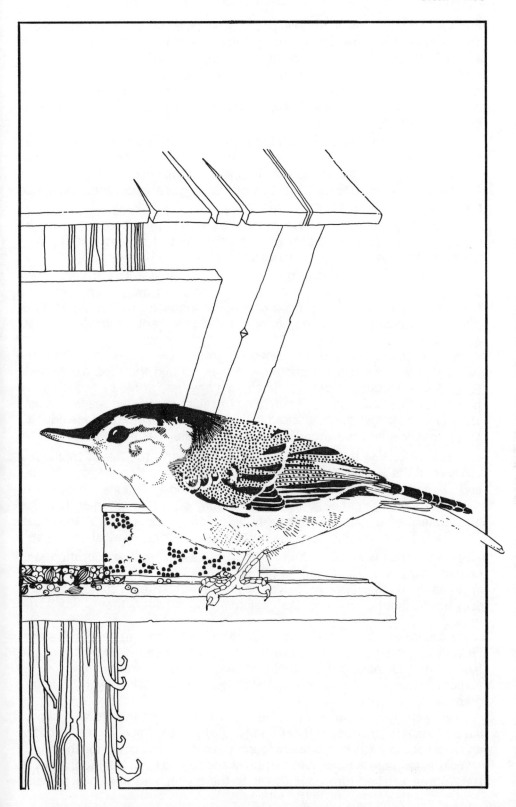

titmice, cardinals, tree sparrows, downy woodpeckers, juncos, starlings and chickadees—that came to the feeder. Once in a while, they were treated by a visit from grosbeaks, goldfinches and mourning doves.

Steve and Ray had built the feeder from scrap lumber. They modeled it from a picture in a book Steve had borrowed from the school library. A hopper feeder, it was called, and it was large enough to house several dinner guests at once.

It was shaped like a house with the front cut away and the roof supported by thick wooden pegs. The builders had put the open front to the east, facing the large picture window on the patio so they could watch the birds coming and going. Because the covered back faced west, the feeder was protected from the wind and snow, too.

Inside, they mounted a triangular-shaped bin to the back wall with hinges. A slight crack along the bottom edge allowed seed to spill out onto the floor. Here, the feeding birds scooped it up.

They had nailed the feeder to a fence post mounted in the ground. Steve and his uncle were careful to locate it in the open away from trees and bushes. Otherwise, neighborhood cats might ambush the feeding birds. A piece of tin wired around the bottom of the post kept squirrels and cats away, too.

Using a small broom, Steve reached high and swept the snow from the roof and inside the feeding station. He then refilled the feed trough with seed. A well-stocked feeder should contain a variety of food since different birds like different kinds of food. Small grains, sunflower seeds, cracked corn, grit and cracked nuts were all included in Steve's mixture. He added a couple of slices of stale bread and filled the water basin in the corner.

Then he checked the bag of suet he had wired to the beech tree a few yards from Jet's snow-covered dog house. The black dog wagged his tail and whined all the while Steve stocked the feeder. Ellen's butcher had given Steve a large chunk of fat. This he dumped inside an onion bag that his mother had donated. Some birds, like downy woodpeckers, love suet. They take turns hanging onto the netting and pecking away at the treat.

Uncle Ray had been helpful in setting up Steve's feeding operation, and he had only one word of caution to his nephew.

"Feed the birds every day, Steve," he had said. "They'll come to depend on your handouts, and you can't let them down when they need it the most."

The feeder restocked, Steve shovelled the snow from the patio and steps. He rolled with Jet in the new snow for a while and then fed and watered the friendly dog. By now, darkness was coming, and the powdery snow took on a slight bluish tint. The wind had stopped, and the white world seemed ghostlike and unreal.

Steve went indoors and, while he waited for his mother to call him to supper, watched the feeder for any activity. It was too close to dark, though, and most of the birds had already found a roost in thick cover for the night.

Looking for a quick meal, a red squirrel popped up from behind the beech tree. Steve watched him bound over to the feeder and snatch a piece of cracked corn that had spilled to the ground. He sat back on his hind feet and nibbled the tidbit.

Steve watched the little squirrel paw through the snow for more grain. Then, without warning, the red squirrel looked up and froze in fear.

It all happened so fast that Steve had trouble reshaping the scene for his family a moment later. A quick rush of white wings followed, and a large, thick-headed white bird with fierce yellow eyes dropped from the darkening sky. It scooped up the squirrel in powerful claws.

Steve had never seen anything like it, especially right here in his own backyard. Uncle Ray had told him often that death in the out-of-doors can be swift and violent. That must be true because the squirrel never knew what had attacked him. He was grabbed quickly and silently, and the bird's claws struck deep in death. The white owl silently flew off toward the river with its prey dangling from vise-like claws.

Steve hollered for his uncle and excitedly told Ray what had happened.

"What was it, Uncle Ray?" the boy asked in wide-eyed wonder.

Ray looked at the wing prints in the fresh snow outside. "Had to be a snowy owl, Steve, an Arctic owl," his uncle said, himself now excited at the thought. "They migrate south when the north country is bitter cold and the snow is deep. They don't know enough about humans to be afraid of them. A local great horned owl, for example, probably wouldn't have taken the chance so close to the house."

He then explained to Steve that many Arctic owls are shot during such years of bad weather since they have no fear of man.

"It's against the law to kill them," Ray told his nephew, "but that doesn't stop some people from trying.

"You just saw a rare sight. I wish I could have gotten that on film."

"It happened so fast, Uncle Ray," Steve said, still excited, "that I would have forgotten to snap the shutter." That night Steve lay awake in bed a long time and thought about what had happened.

The next morning dawned silent and white and cold. Sitta, the nuthatch, stirred inside the small knothole in the maple where she lived, halfway down the slope to the river behind Ellen's house. She thrust her head outdoors to survey the silent blanket of snow. Seeing no danger, she flitted to a nearby branch. She peeped a morning song, and somewhere near the river her mate answered.

Twice during the night she and other sleeping birds along the tree-covered slope were awakened by the fearful booming of Bubo, the great horned owl. Like the others, she shrank into her den and trembled at the night hunter's sounds. But with the growing light of day came safety, and now the little bird felt hungry. She had pecked at a few beech buds the night before but had not had a full meal in two days because of the storm. She danced from tree to tree and checked for insects while clinging to the bark upside down as nuthatches do.

About half again as big as a sparrow or chickadee, Sitta was a handsome bird. Her upper plumage was blue-gray. She sported a snow-white belly and face, topped with black, button-like eyes, a sharp ebony beak and black cap.

Working her way from tree to tree up the hill, she remembered the bird feeder. When she arrived, the feeder was already a flurry of activity. A pair of bright red cardinals picked out the choice sunflower seeds, and several starlings gobbled up grain as fast as they could peck. Nearby in bare branches, a tufted titmouse and several English sparrows waited for their turns.

The feeder had given Sitta many easy meals during this harsh winter and, like the other birds, she had come to depend upon it for her survival. She flitted to a nearby limb. Not wanting to scrap with the larger, more aggressive birds, she awaited her turn at the station.

Sudden movement behind the patio door glass frightened the feeding birds into flight. Sitta paused a moment and then flew to the feeder. She dropped to the platform and began pecking away at some of the smaller seeds.

She saw the faces of Steve and his sister, but was too hungry to be frightened away. The children, dressed in their sleepwear, sat cross-legged behind the glass and cradled cups of hot chocolate in their hands.

"That sure is a funny looking bird," Theresa said to her brother and pointed at Sitta.

"That's the nuthatch," Steve said. "She's been coming here longer than any others."

Ray came down from his upstairs bedroom and watched for a moment. "You kids can learn more about wildlife by getting involved, as you are right now, than from any book," he said. "I wish I could watch the birds with you, but I have to get in to the university."

For two hours they watched the birds come and go at the feeder. They saw the bully blue jay chase Sitta away, and they watched how the cardinals cracked open sunflower seeds with their strong beaks. A pair of downy woodpeckers took turns punching at the bag of suet and an evening grosbeak made a brief appearance.

By 10 o'clock, most of the birds had finished their morning's meal, and Steve and Theresa got dressed to go outside and play.

CHAPTER 19

the Crow

 hortly after dawn one February morning, a large, black bird quietly flew into the branches of a towering beech tree. This small grove of leafless trees overlooked Riverside Subdivision. It gave Corvus, the crow, a fine view of the snow-packed road and the suburban homes with their look-alike, snow-blanketed roofs.

Corvus had perched in this same tree on cold mornings before, and with his excellent eyesight had sometimes found scraps of food to eat in the neighborhood.

In the silent distance Corvus faintly heard one of his black comrades calling in deep crow tones. Corvus replied with three loud caws of his own, which started a neighborhood dog barking. Soon the passing crow dropped to a nearby branch, and after a few moments a third crow joined them.

A half hour earlier the crows had fanned out from their roost in thick woods across the river near the farmers' fields, but food was hard to find in such deep snow and cold weather. During such hard times crows often team up to find something to eat.

The three crows puffed up their breast feathers against the cold. They shifted their weight from one foot to another as the freezing air numbed them. A cheerless sun, screened behind a gray cloud layer, brought full daylight with it. After a time, the crows watched garage doors open and heard engines starting in the neighborhood below. Exhaust hung like thick smoke in the still morning air.

Soon, children emptied from the houses and began to crowd around the bus stop.

"Look at those dirty crows," one of the boys said, pointing with a

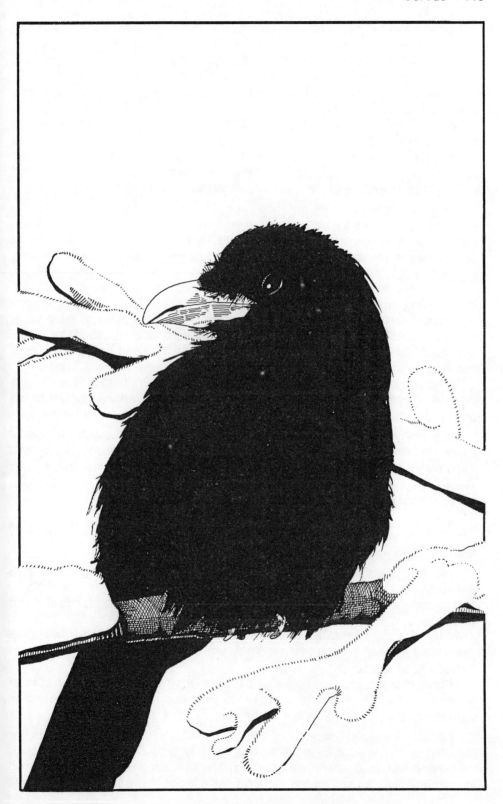

mittened hand to the three black figures in the beech. "How'd you like to shoot all three of them?" he asked the others.

"My dad hunts crows," Jerry said, his wide cheeks pinker than usual this morning. "He says they're smart and hard to shoot."

"So what? They're still good for nothing," the other boy added. "I mean, really, have you ever eaten a crow?"

"Well, I don't know what good they are, but my dad thinks they're neat to hunt," Jerry said in defense.

From their high perches, Corvus and the others watched the yellow school bus crunch to a halt next to the milling students. The children boarded quickly and the conversation soon changed to upcoming events at school.

Many people hate crows because they think they are no good. To many, the crow is nature's bad guy, and he is on a lot of people's nuisance lists. Like other animals with sometimes bad reputations, such as snakes or predators like the hawks, owls and foxes, the crow seems to do more wrong than good.

To farmers, he is a crop destroyer, and scarecrows and noisemakers will not keep him out of spring fields or fall berry patches. To bird lovers, he is a murderer that destroys a tremendous number of songbirds' eggs each year. Farther north in the prairie potholes of Canada, where thousands of ducks nest each spring, he kills many of their young in the shell before they ever hatch.

The crow has been branded a pirate, a freebooter, a murderer and a nuisance for many years. In the past, some states even had bounties on crows, and farmers have long welcomed crow hunters on their property.

Over many years, wide open seasons and the use of electronic game callers began to cut into crow numbers. In some cases, nonsportsmen and even angry farmers have shot into the roosts at night. Then the birds can't see to fly, and hundreds could be killed at a time. There have even been times when crows were dynamited as they slept.

Most states now have controlled hunting seasons. For the most part, populations are staying the same. In some areas, though, there probably never will be enough crows to cause nuisance problems again.

Few people stop to think that the crow is a challenging gamebird to hunters. Very smart and wary birds, crows are almost impossible to stalk, and most hunters use decoys, blinds and calls just as they do for ducks and geese.

Another feature that people overlook is that, as scavengers, crows eat a great deal of dead animal matter. They are nature's garbagemen and help to keep roadways clean.

Although crows may do many bad things, they are an important part of the environment. Every living thing in the outdoors, no matter how useless or damaging it may seem, serves a purpose.

Unable to find food today in the neighborhood, the black trio flew on lazily flapping wings toward Bellecrest village. They would look for a car-struck rabbit or other dead animal on the road. Then they would scour the parking lots around the village for scraps of food and check out the year-around drive-in for scattered popcorn. Like Meph, the skunk, Corvus and the other crows were omnivorous.

It was late forenoon when the crows finally satisfied their hunger for the time being. Not until late afternoon would they begin to filter together in trees along the river. It has long been a crow custom for the birds to gang together in such afternoon gathering points a mile or so from their roosts.

After a day of looking for food that might take them 50 miles from the roost, the crows come in from all compass points like ragged, black strings. Then they generally make a lot of racket, as crows are very sociable birds. A listener might think they were chatting back and forth about the things they saw and did in their travels that day. Then, just before dark, they lift up as a large body and silently fly to the roost where they wait out the long, cold winter night.

Crows are lazy, and Corvus and the others had several hours until they would group together. So they flew slowly downriver to find some mischief to get into or some other tidbit to eat.

Just a couple of hundred yards below Riverside Subdivision the river made a sharp bend. It was here on the other side of the river that the sharp-eyed Corvus spotted his most hated and feared enemy.

Bubo, the great horned owl, was sleeping on an oak limb after a night of successful hunting. Deep in the hardwoods behind him, his mate sat tightly to their clutch of two large, white eggs. She, too, had eaten, and Bubo had no cares at the moment. Little did he realize that his troubles were about to begin.

The second Corvus spotted the hulking, grey-brown owl, he uttered some frantic **caws.** To the others strung out behind him, he might have said, "Hey, guys, look what I found! Here's something we can tease!"

When the other two crows spotted Bubo, they joined in the fray. Bubo cocked open one large yellow eye and studied the situation. He was not afraid of the noisy crows and, in fact, could tear them to pieces if he wanted to. But he was a bird of night, and the daytime world of noise and brightness bothered him. He opened both eyes as the screaming crows dive-bombed him. The light brought pain to his great yellow eyes, and Bubo blinked hard a couple of times.

He was annoyed with the crows and their rudeness. One darted by him so closely that it screamed in the owl's ear. Bubo clicked his powerful beak at the black streak. Other crows soon heard the trouble and began to move upriver and downriver toward the action that Corvus had found.

Soon a dozen crows swarmed over the owl's head, and the noise was becoming too much for Bubo. Backed by his cheering comrades, Corvus grew even more bold. He swept down hard and pecked at the owl's great, thick head. Bubo hissed loudly and snapped his beak at this invader who dared to touch him.

Finally, the owl had had enough. He dropped from the limb, and on those powerful wings began to make his way downriver where the woods grew even thicker. Maybe he could lose the noisy troublemakers in a dense woodlot. The crow pack strung out behind and over him and cawed and pecked away at the larger bird.

Crows and owls hate each other and are mortal enemies. At night, the woods and black skies belong to the owls who fly on silent wings. They have been known to kill crows and destroy their eggs while the birds sit on the nests. But in daytime, the crow has the upper hand, and there is little an angry owl can do except hide from these black rascals.

Bubo slid into some heavy cover where the trees grew thickly together. But Corvus and his gang of black pests followed him right in and kept up their attacks. After a minute or two, Bubo again took to the air with the string of loud crows right behind him.

But the owl had another trick that had worked before when all else failed. This time, instead of fleeing downriver, Bubo shot for the sky. He could fly at great heights, if he had to, to get away from the crows. They followed him for a while and then began dropping off one by one. Cawing all the way, Corvus stayed with the escaping owl. Higher and higher the pair flew until they were dim specks against the gray sky. Finally Corvus, too, gave up the chase and drifted downward to his friends.

Meanwhile, Bubo leveled off at nearly a half mile above the black and white earth. At this great height he soared for a long while and studied the expanse of woods and fields below. He could see the twisting river as it wound its black, snakelike body through Westwind Woods.

On each side of the river he could see the woods as they parted like coarse hair before a comb. He looked at the white and brown barren fields that stretched from the river to the toylike clusters of farm buildings. Traffic inched along the dark road strips on both sides of the tract, and Bubo could see the buildings and houses that formed Bellecrest village. With sight grown used to the brightness by now, the owl eyed the dim outline of Gratiot City as the factory town hunched above the horizon, miles to the east.

The scene below was almost as though someone had neatly designed it on paper and shaded in the right mixture of black, gray, brown and white. Where the town of Bellecrest stopped, the woods began, and the farmers' fields were neatly drawn with straight fence rows cutting them at proper angles.

Little did Bubo know that this might be his last look at Westwind Woods as it now appeared. The election day of March 10, which would decide once and for all the fate of the natural tract, loomed more closely each day.

Below him, across the county in the world of people, the upcoming election was a constant topic. People talked about the merits of the lake proposal and the merits of leaving Westwind Woods as it was and the cost to do both. They argued about it in the factories of Gratiot City as production workers stamped out car parts. Shoppers discussed it in supermarkets as did teachers and their students and merchants and their customers.

Whenever people came together—at church, at bingo games, at sports events and at social gatherings—the subject of Westwind Woods came up. Newscasters talked about it on the evening news. Newspapers ran daily articles about what the various groups were doing to make voters see their side.

The conservation clubs' point of view was simple and direct. Destroy Westwind Woods and waste a tremendous natural resource. They pointed to the Environmental Impact Study as evidence that the ecology would suffer if a lake were created. In meetings large and small across the county, the conservation people told about the efforts of many citizens to protect natural resources. They explained that this was the one chance that county residents had to protect the last wild tract they owned.

Billboards and ads in newspapers and on radio and television told of the pride that Bellecrest County citizens could take in the project to save Westwind Woods. It could become a state and maybe even a national victory for ecology. Mr. Reynolds and many others worked hard to get the people behind saving Westwind Woods.

On the university campus in Gratiot City, Ray helped put together debates on the subject. In his classroom, students organized a "Save Westwind Woods" committee to take the message to the voters. A large amount of money was needed to pay for the advertising. But donations were slow in coming. The farmers' groups, local 4-H clubs, Boy Scouts and private donations helped

The people behind the lake project had money and were just as eager to have the man-made lake become real. They told of the need for county recreation sites, especially for the citizens of Gratiot City. They produced figures and charts to show that such a lake would be used a great deal.

The backers of the lake plan were mostly Bellecrest village merchants. They had already formed themselves into a local chamber of commerce and were planning for happy years ahead. The mayor of Bellecrest village and the mayor of Gratiot City made a joint statement that the lake was something the citizens sorely needed.

These were tough foes to defeat. Mr. Reynolds, Ray and the other volunteers knew they had an uphill fight if they were going to win the election. The powerful union in Gratiot City withheld its support for either side. Both the lake backers and the Save Westwind Woods committee agreed that union support was important for their side to win. Finally, a few days before the election, the union's board of directors said that it would make no decision in the matter. It told its thousands of members to vote as they wished as both projects had merit.

This was neither a victory nor a defeat for the conservation people, but it summed up the problem. Voters had mixed feelings on this subject. They would not be swayed by facts and figures but would vote how they felt at the moment.

So far, both sides, for the most part, had stayed away from emotions and had tried to present their arguments with logic and fact.

But all that changed when Ardea, the great blue heron, returned to Westwind Woods when March was only a couple of days old.

CHAPTER 20

ARDEA
the Great Blue Heron

 he came in the night on powerful wings that carried her north on a flight of few stops from her wintering grounds in the southern United States. She could easily have rested several times at waterfowl refuges along her route. In recent days, hundreds of ducks and geese had been dropping in to the refuge a hundred miles south of Westwind Woods. They were waiting for ice-out and the last legs of their spring migrations.

But Ardea headed straight for Westwind Woods, the only home she had ever known other than her winter quarters in the southern marshes.

And in the north country winter had hung on stubbornly. During the last couple of hours of her northern trip, sleet stung her face and glazed her feathers. Far below, the winter world looked dark and hostile. Street lights and neon signs of the towns and villages winked as the night migrator passed over in silent flight.

At dawn, patchy snow partly blanketed Westwind Woods. Ardea dropped her wings low and curved her crooked neck even more to make a landing. She chose a shallow area of the pond and was surprised when she skidded out of control upon contact with the ice.

No one fully understands the instinct that causes some birds to migrate. Some experts claim that the urge to reproduce themselves is the reason. Others believe that the sun, moon and stars are responsible. Some say that weather changes are the biggest factor.

Ardea did not know why she would fly in the middle of the night through a sleet storm to return to such a barren land. Neither could she tell how she knew to return to the exact place year after year. A strong, mysterious force,

begun thousands of years ago by generations of herons before, drove her north each spring.

She had returned this year too early, and little did she know that food would be hard to find in the winter-coated world. The frogs and crayfish that Ardea liked to eat slept away the cold in numb hibernation. They lay buried in the mud bottom of the pond and river. A final spring breakup was still nearly two weeks away, and the tall, blue-gray bird on stilt-like legs would have to search hard for food.

Maybe she had returned early in hopes of finding a mate this spring. Like Taxus, the badger, Ardea had lost her mate. Because no other herons lived in Westwind Woods, she had been unable to replace him.

The death of Ardea's mate in the late summer two years ago had been a real loss. Each morning, the male heron had had a habit of flying to a shallow lake and marsh a couple miles away. One day, he did not return. Although Ardea never knew why, his death was due to a killer disease called botulism.

Botulism is a killer that has nothing to do with man. Without warning, it can occur in the environment and kill large numbers of waterfowl and marsh birds like the herons. It attacks the nervous system and paralyzes its victims. Botulism always ends in death. Its effect on birds can be just as deadly as a chemical or oil spill.

Late one summer afternoon, Steve and some of the other boys had found the heron's body by the marsh and reported their find to Ray. The heron's death posed a real problem for Ray. He took a few pictures of the bird and searched the area for other dead wildlife. From skin tissues cut from the dead bird, a state biologist and Ray found evidence of botulism. This same disease has killed many ducks and shorebirds a short distance away.

All of this knowledge, of course, did not help bring Ardea's mate back to her. And although the sleet let up by full daylight, the drab brown and white world of Westwind Woods was not much of a homecoming for the lone heron, either. During this first day home in early March, she spent the hours walking the river shallows where some open water might produce something to eat.

Meanwhile, the election that would decide the fate of Westwind Woods was only a week away. Bellecrest County people were still being told of its importance. Radio and television programs often were interrupted by advertisements for or against the lake plan. A letter asking voters to save the woods and fields was mailed to all families. This mailing by the conservation people was quickly followed by a letter from the merchants' group. They once more told of the need for county recreation and asked for a "yes" vote for the lake.

Never in the county had such an issue gotten so much attention. The conservation groups were staking their very reputations on March 10, when 75 percent of the voters were expected to cast ballots. A bumper sticker campaign was working for the conservation people. "Save Westwind Woods on March 10" slogans in red, white and blue were showing up on many cars.

The merchants came back with yard signs in eye-catching yellow and black posters. "Make Westwind Lake a dream come true—vote 'yes' for county recreation on March 10," was the message they carried.

Polls showed that with a week to go before the election, most voters were well informed. The vote promised to be close, too close to predict a winner.

Along with many others on both sides, Ray began to feel the pressure of the hard fight. For several weeks, he had worked late into the night, knocking on people's doors to talk with them and meeting with committees to plan their attack. The closer March 10 appeared, the more tired he felt. The ungraded papers from his university classes began to mount, and Ray was worn out.

On the afternoon of Ardea's return, he drove slowly back from his last class at the university to his sister's home. He had planned to lie down and catch a long nap before supper but decided instead to take a hike into the woods.

He knew this would refresh him as much as sleep. He had spent much time in the outdoors. His experiences with the quiet and natural beauty of the woods and fields had usually helped to straighten out his thinking and recharge his energies when he had a problem or needed a boost.

Slipping on jeans and a wool shirt over insulated underwear, Ray added his rubber felt pacs for footwear and an olive drab, hooded parka. He never went into the woods without his photography equipment. He carefully packed a 35 mm camera, tripod, wide angle lens and telephoto lens with several cartons of film into his blaze orange packsack.

By midafternoon, he was walking along the twisting footpath that flanked the Kenawabi River. He noticed maroon buds that peppered the outer branches of the iron gray beech trees and knew that in a few weeks they would sprout bunches of bright green leaves. Muskrat tracks along the river showed that these animals were on the move as late winter is the beginning of their mating season.

There was little that the trained wildlife teacher missed. A lifetime of following outdoor interests and two university degrees had prepared him well for an understanding and appreciation of the natural world. He saw the red breast of a robin as it flew through the undergrowth. Ray wondered if the bird was an early returnee from warmer climates or a refugee of the hard winter now passing.

If people only knew and understood the outdoors, they would help to save these woods from destruction, Ray thought to himself. Each time a marsh was filled to make way for more homes or a river dammed and valuable woods flooded, more than just wildlife and plantlife suffered. In time, the human population would suffer, too.

Long ago, Ray decided that his life's work would be to help others understand and enjoy the outdoors. Already this walk, through wet March woods at the drabbest time of year, began to provide the tonic Ray needed. He thought about his work and about his stand against the lake plan and he knew that he was right.

His boots crunched on ice shards along the path, and the cool, fresh wind felt good on his face. Plunging deeper into the woods, he soon came to the clearing where the marsh began. He pushed through the alder tangle where

Philo, the woodcock, had nested last spring and then paused at the still frozen marsh edge.

Ray sat on a smooth, white stone for a long while and thought about things and the directions they were going. As afternoon deepened, the evening chill came early, and Ray snuggled deeper into his parka and pulled the hood over his head. Once he thought he caught a glimpse of a fox across the meadow. The animal's rusty brown coat was probably too light to be the cross fox he had photographed last summer and was probably a brother or sister of Vulpes, Ray figured. A ragged ribbon-like band of crows fluttered from the sky above him and moved slowly downriver.

"You black devils," Ray laughed aloud. "I'll bet you still have that roost in the pines downriver, don't you?"

And then Ray saw another movement near the river a quarter mile away. He strained hard, squinting his eyes to see better in the failing light and caught movement again, a little blur of blue-gray. Ray snapped the telephoto lens to his camera and focused the object into view.

"It's the blue heron!" he said to himself. "I can't believe she's back this early." Quickly, Ray loaded his camera with high speed color slide film and secured his camera to a tripod.

Unaware of the man in the marsh, Ardea walked slowly toward Ray. She had been lucky to find a few mussels in the soft river bottom mud and had satisfied her hunger for this day. Now she wanted a dry place to sleep away the cold night.

Ray began snapping pictures of the approaching heron when Ardea was about 200 yards away. The tall bird took long, careful steps toward him. Taking care to conceal his movement by squatting in the marsh, Ray moved the camera a little to his left to get in more of a spreading, blood-red sunset as background.

Suddenly, Ardea took one last cautious step and then stopped. She cocked her large head from left to right and then turned sideways for a moment and stretched her great neck straight up to the sky. She had heard the click of Ray's camera shutter but could not determine its source. Ardea shifted an impatient foot each time she heard the strange clicking sound and began to grow frightened. Once, she spread her wide wings as though to fly but changed her mind and folded them back to her body.

Ardea looked carefully into the marsh but could see nothing other than the straw-colored cattails and the dark earth mounds of muskrat houses. To her, the man appeared as just another clump of vegetation. She took another couple of dainty steps and then caught a definite movement as the photographer shifted his arm.

Instantly, Ardea took to the air with a loud squawk. Ray quickly unscrewed his camera from the tripod and followed her upward flight with a couple of snaps. The great bird flew slowly upriver for a moment or two. Then she banked west and journeyed downriver toward the crow roost. Ray took two or three dramatic last shots of the regal heron, neck crooked in an S shape and feet trailing behind, an impressive silhouette against the red-stained sky.

Ray knew that what he had captured on film was rare. Many times in the past he had paid no attention to mosquitoes or numbing cold to get the outdoor pictures he wanted. The file in his bedroom at Ellen's house was bulging with photos from Westwind Woods taken over the years, but he could not recall ever seeing a sight so grand. He hoped he was able to get it on film.

His pants were soaked from kneeling in the marsh, but Ray did not notice, nor would he care if he knew. He stuffed the camera equipment into his pack and shouldered it to begin the long hike home.

And then the full impact of a tremendous idea hit him.

"That's it! Of course, that's it! Why didn't I think of it sooner?" he said aloud.

Ray ran much of the two miles back to Riverside Subdivision. He burst in the door and asked his sister to keep supper warm for an hour or so until he could return.

"Ray, what's going on?" Ellen wanted to know.

"I've got to run this film over to Jay's Studio," Ray shot back through the open door. "I'll tell you when I get back."

Later that evening after a quick supper, Ray searched his file cabinet and pulled out all the slides of animals and plants he had photographed over the years. Steve helped him sort the best pictures of foxes, ducks, geese, deer, flowers, trees and others.

Satisfied that he had the right photos, Ray got on the phone to Mr. Reynolds.

"Don, can we find a few hundred dollars for a television ad?" Ray wanted to know. "I've got an idea here that should win us the election hands down."

"I don't know, Ray. We're in debt now," Mr. Reynolds said. "What do you have?"

"I'd rather show you than tell you, Don. Can you and the committee members be here tomorrow night at 7?"

"Sure," Mr. Reynolds said. "But give me a clue."

"I'm going to give you a sneak preview of a great television ad I'm putting together, but I've got to have some help on writing and editing the copy," Ray explained. "I'll have it ready, at least in rough form, by tomorrow evening."

"I can't wait to see it," Mr. Reynolds said. "We'll be there tomorrow night."

CHAPTER 21

the
RECKONING

he next morning, Ray picked up the slides of Ardea that he had taken the evening before. A teacher friend and two of Ray's students helped him put the best ones in order and write copy for a television message which they tested over and over on a tape recorder.

That night after supper, several members of the conservation club met in the living room of Ellen's home while Ray set up a slide projector and screen and prepared the tape.

When everything was ready, Ray began, "This is what I'd like to put on television over the next couple of days as many times as we can afford to do it."

Ray focused the first slide, a beautiful, sweeping scene of the green meadow in Westwind Woods. He adjusted the sound on his tape recorder, and a man's voice began:

"By now, you surely know about the election next Monday to decide whether Westwind Woods will be stripped of its natural beauty and turned into a man-made lake."

Little beeps in the soundtrack were cues for Ray to advance new slides. Each one of the marsh, pond, fields and woodlots was breathtaking in its beauty.

The voice on the tape went on, "Most of us already have decided how we'll vote, but how many of us really know what treasures Westwind Woods holds? Let's take a close-up look and see."

The slides switched from landscape scenes to stunning close range shots of flower, trees, birds and animals. Vulpes played on a hillside with the

other fox pups. There was a dramatic picture of Branta, his mate and a brood of a half-dozen goslings. Odo grazed in the meadow, his massive rack of horns spread wide in summer velvet.

The slide parade of animals and birds went on, and the speaker began to talk about the proposed lake. He admitted that it would benefit people but also warned of how so much valuable plantlife and animal life would be destroyed. The message to save Westwind Woods was clear. Ray's excellent slides began to drive home this point. Ray glanced around the room and could tell from the committee members' faces that they liked what they were seeing and hearing.

The voice then recalled Colonel West's early efforts at conservation. A picture of his old white mansion appeared on the screer , and the narrator said, "Do you think the colonel would have wanted thése beautiful woods destroyed and its wild creatures killed?"

"Westwind Woods used to be home for this pair of great blue herons," the speaker said, referring to Ardea and her former mate. "There was a time when herons were plentiful in this area, but human progress—in the form of homes and highways, industries and urban sprawl—has cut into their numbers."

A picture of the dead male appeared, and the voice said, "And then the male heron died from botulism, a disease that paralyzes birds. Now only the female is left."

Ray's most recent picture of Ardea, a stunning black figure against the blood-red sky, came into view.

"These pictures of the female heron were taken on March 3, probably the day she returned from her wintering grounds in the Deep South," the speaker said. "She may very well be the last great blue heron in Bellecrest County. We must preserve her habitat—indeed, the habitat of all these birds and animals. Vote 'No' on the lake proposal on March 10."

The screen glared white when Ray removed this last slide, and the room began to hum with talk. Ray shut off the projector and turned on the living room lights. "Gentlemen," he asked, "what do you think?"

"Tremendous, Ray, just tremendous," Mr. Reynolds said, slowly shaking his head in wonder. "This should help us win it for sure!"

"Best idea we've had yet," another member said. "I'm sure we can come up with the money for a TV ad."

Another added, "I just don't see how people can vote against keeping the woods, especially after seeing this."

A fourth member wanted to know if Ray had shot all the slides himself and if they were taken in Westwind Woods. "If so," he said, "I think we should mention it as it could make the ad even better."

"Good point," Ray agreed. "What we need now is some more ideas like that."

The members talked about ways to improve the presentation. One idea was to remind voters at the end to say "Yes" to the request for one mill of tax to support recreation in the county. Another was to say that this new money could help toward building a man-made lake elsewhere. The money could also be used to help develop Westwind Woods into nature trails, to build a nature interpretation center and to pay for patrol officers to stop poaching.

Armed with the committee's support and fresh ideas, Ray took the slides and tape recording to the television station in Gratiot City early the next morning. Within two days, the message was being broadcast throughout the region.

It played a big part in changing many people's thinking. The merchants had no hard-hitting, last minute plan of their own to counter this new threat. As these final days before the election passed, a growing number of voters decided to cast their ballots against the lake plan.

On the evening of March 10 when the votes were counted, the Save Westwind Woods Committee won by a whopping 2-1 margin! The millage request passed also, though only slightly.

That night, Steve was allowed to stay up late to watch the special election returns with his Uncle Ray who was overjoyed with the victory.

The phone rang, and Steve scooted to the kitchen to answer it before it awakened the rest of the family. Returning to the living room, Steve said, "Uncle Ray, it's for you. It's Mr. Reynolds."

The two men talked excitedly like children with new toys. "There's just no question about it, Ray," Mr. Reynolds said. "You're the hero of the hour. If it hadn't been for your idea, I don't think we would have won it. Thanks to you, we won, and we won big."

"Everybody worked hard, Don. You know that. It was just a lucky thought I had in the marsh that day."

"Just the same," Mr. Reynolds went on, "you proved to a lot of people that you really know Westwind Woods inside out. I still can't get over the extent of your photo file on that area."

"Well, I've been tramping around there ever since I was a kid," Ray said.

"I know you have," Mr. Reynolds said. "I'm sure the county board is going to appoint a citizens' committee to advise the Parks and Recreation Commission. They're going to need the public's advice on how best to preserve Westwind Woods as well as to develop it with nature trails and so on." Mr. Reynolds paused for a moment.

"I want you to represent us on that committee, Ray," he said.

"Don, there's nothing I'd like to do more."

The pair agreed that Westwind Woods could become one of the finest nature preserves in the state, if not the very finest. After several more minutes of talk, Ray hung up the phone.

"Come on, Steve, let's get to bed," he said. "This is one night I'm going to sleep well."

Over the next few days, winter lost its icy hold on the land. Warm spring rains washed away the last traces of snow and ice by the end of March. By mid-April, the sun shone nearly every day.

Mr. Reynolds' prediction came true, and Ray found himself working hard with a committee from across the county. One afternoon in late April, he found some spare time and went for a hike into Westwind Woods. Steve went with his uncle and listened carefully during their hike along the river as Ray explained some of the committee's plans.

"For one thing, we don't plan any roads at all in here," Ray said.

"How will people get in here then?" Steve wondered.

"Well, of course, there will be several foot trails," Ray said. "And we're going to allow a canoe rental company in town so people can float the Kenawabi River. We're planning to make some picnic areas along scenic take-out spots like over there," Ray gestured.

The two were standing along the river's east bank. Across its brown water, a small, natural clearing began along high banks. It butted up to thick woods whose swollen buds were ready to burst with new leaves any day.

"This might even be a good place for one of the rope bridges that the committee has suggested," Ray said.

The day stayed warm as the pair walked slowly downstream. Ray took some notes on a clipboard he carried. He told Steve of the committee's plan to pay certain farmers across the river to plant corn in the hope of attracting migrating waterfowl.

"What about fishing?" Steve asked.

"Fishing will be allowed on the river," his uncle said, "but not in the pond itself. The pond is home to too many animals and is too delicate for a lot of fishermen to use it."

When they reached the pond, Steve could see what Ray meant. "There's really no way people can get to the pond without breaking through the marsh," Steve said.

"That's exactly the point," Ray agreed. "But we'd like to see at least a nature trail around the marsh. Wetlands like this marsh are fast disappearing in this country. People need to know how important they are, both to us and to the animals alike."

"The marsh and pond are my favorite spots in Westwind Woods, Uncle Ray."

"They've always been mine, too," Ray said.

The marsh was once more alive with spring. Cassidix, the grackle, and a few of his noisy friends watched from the safety of the woods fringe across the pond. Below them in the wet marsh, Ondatra, the muskrat, chewed on tender cattail roots. Although she could not be seen, Philo, the woodcock, had returned and now lay tightly nestled to a new clutch of eggs in the dense alder tangle.

Greening stems of new cattail growth shot upward from the lively marsh, and once more bright yellow cowslips flanked the little stream that trickled away to the river. Across the river freshly tilled fields that soon would sprout new crops again shimmered with the bright setting sun.

In the meadow, green grass was growing tall, Ray noticed, while he and Steve walked across the lush carpet. They walked toward the old West mansion at the meadow's end. Ray pointed out that some camping might be allowed near the house, which itself would be headquarters for running the preserve.

"We're talking of building a nature interpretation center. We'll either build it here near the West house or farther downriver near Grayson Road Bridge,'' Ray said.

''What's a nature interpretation center, Uncle Ray?'' Steve wondered.

''It's a building where people can go in and learn about wild things—how they grow and live and why they are important resources,'' Ray said.

''You mean, displays and pictures and things like that?''

''Right,'' Ray said. ''There will probably be some real mounted animals and short films, too, to explain all these things to people.''

Ray looked a long moment at his nephew, now almost 13 years old and not really a little boy anymore. Steve's eyes were the same bright blue as always and his blonde bangs forever graced his forehead, but the childlike expression was somehow nearly gone. Some of the freckles still spattered Steve's cheeks and the frail chin and slender nose were unchanged. Yet his overall appearance was becoming more adult than child.

The West mansion loomed before them as a white, ghostlike blur in the growing twilight. The two sat quietly on the old, wooden steps of the front porch, and Steve peeled a loose strip of paint from one of the thick round pillars. Otus called to his mate across the meadow in that strange tone that only screech owls produce. From the corner of his eye, Ray watched a bat chasing insects in the darkening sky. A waft of warm air with heavy spring smells floated by.

Steve held a piece of peeled paint between his fingers and began chipping it into little pieces with a fingernail. ''Uncle Ray,'' he said looking up, ''do you think the world will ever be destroyed?''

''That's a pretty heavy question, Steve. What do you mean?''

''I mean, with nuclear bombs and food shortages in some places and wars in other places and crime getting worse everywhere, I just wonder if this world can take all these problems and survive,'' Steve explained.

His uncle was silent for a long moment. ''I don't have the answer to that one, Steve,'' he said finally. ''But I do know that each of us must try hard to better the world in any way we can.''

Steve broke in, ''That's why you worked hard to save Westwind Woods, isn't it, Uncle Ray?''

''That's right,'' Ray said. ''If people can't respect their own environment, how can they ever respect the rights of others? Your generation must keep up what my generation has finally started to do—to protect our natural resources. To stop damming the rivers, filling the marshes and polluting the lakes and streams. We have to work hard on this for a very good reason, Steve.''

''What do you mean?''

''Well,'' Ray began, ''the natural world stands as a living wall between us and extinction. I mean, if the environment can't keep a wild population alive, how can it keep alive a human one?'' Ray paused to see if Steve was catching the meaning of what he said.

Satisfied, Ray went on, ''The plants and animals give us a constant check as to how we're doing with air pollution, water pollution and living space. When they're healthy, we know we're healthy, too. The other side is also true. If a chemical spill in a river kills fish, we know that the water is probably unsafe for us, too. Do you understand why the wild things are important to us?''

"Yes," Steve said, "I think I do now even better."

Night had come to Westwind Woods. After a moment, Steve said, "I suppose Ma will worry if we don't get back soon."

"You're right; I guess we better go," Ray said. "We can take the highway home if you want to—it's a lot faster."

"Can we walk along the river?" Steve asked. "I'll bet the spring peepers are out tonight."

A big smile spread across Ray's face. "Yes," he said, "let's walk home along the river."